Dear Corinne, Robbie, & Family,
In gratitude for our friendship.
Wishing you lots of happiness.
Love,
Lydia

Forward

These writings show the insights unique to men and women

in enlightened stages of life.

When we meet as a group of writers, something magical happens.

We listen and respond to each other with

understanding, appreciation and encouragement.

And now, we invite you to enter into our

Magic Room

Introduction

The Magic Room is a book of poetry and prose by eleven writers who live in The Fairways at Lake Ridge, Lakewood, an active adult residential community in Ocean County, New Jersey.

They come together as a group of writers, meeting monthly, to share their writing and to encourage and support each other. Through the years of meeting an undeniable bond has been formed and their work is of great depth and insight. All of them agree that each time they meet; it is like coming into a magic room of fellowship, trust and compassion.

We hope that others will enjoy the work presented here and glean some added insight into life's progression as the writers have.

Contents

Contributors

Rosalie Auerbach.	Pages 4 - 13
Lydia Bargiuk.	Pages 14 - 24
Phil de Anguera.	Pages 25 - 45
Marygene Fagan.	Pages 46 - 59
Patrick Gatton.	Pages 60 - 92
Elaine Grassi.	Pages 93 - 106
Fran Karnish.	Pages 107 - 113
Barbara Pastorello.	Pages 114 - 131
Joan Saunders.	Pages 132 - 158
Marion Stavitsky.	Pages 159 - 166
Anise Singer.	Pages 167 - 182

Rosalie Auerbach

To write is to breathe

A Place Within my Heart

If I could find a place within my heart
That would hold all that there is to fear
      And cocoon the hurts and anger of life
        Perhaps all would be better

If I could find a place within my heart
That would keep safe the memories of happy times
      That are not to be forgotten and bring them back for comfort

If I could find a place within my heart
      To hold the sorrows that constrict and overflow
      Perhaps I'd heal and hurt no more

If I could find a place within my heart
      To hold the goodness of life
      Then my life would shine from within

If I could find a place within my heart
      To keep me whole and the future safe
      Then all that is cherished would be secure

If I could only find a place in my heart.

Essence

Somewhere within
The deep recesses of my being
There's a place that holds my dreams
No guarantees are given by this secret source
Each wish and dream remains alive waiting to be born
Into the reality of breath
I don't have to voice these essences for
They are grounded in my life
They are the core of all people who wish and dream
Without them life has no purpose
I cradle them within and give birth to them when their season has come
Flowering into reality
It is then that my dreams can flourish.

Metamorphosis

The waters flow and churn
Each ripple an individual heaving forward to join the watery world
Storms arise, tossing and forming the ripples into waves.
Such is life
The ebb and surge of a liquid
Moving one from ripple to wave
From the pinnacles to the depths.

Take me out of the swirling waters and set me gently on the sand
I have been clothed by the foam and swallowed the noxious waters
Set me on the cool sand
Where my troubles can recede with each retreating ripple of the waters
There I can sit quietly and breath the free air that will diffuse my being
For I don't want to be me
Let me emerge and arise anew.

Son of my son

Son of my son
Removed from my breast
But not once removed from my heart

Were you mine
Our worlds would change
You would look to me for all that is
But- Now I must stand aside
For-You are not mine
      To feed
      To hold
      To teach

There are moments
These moments are few
They quickly disperse
Consumed by the fear
That you are not mine
You are the son of my son

Seasonal

Days whisper by in a melody of colors
Summer's halo of golden brilliance
Autumnal's lengthening shadows of deeper hues
Tender snowflakes of winter's white
To spring's renaissance of nature's resonating palette
Telescoping on the rainbow of time
Speaking without words
Only the cacophony of hues
Transforming in a burgeoning array
Life's continuum
The exquisiteness reinforced by the deliciousness of
Repetitive change
Always the same
Always different
Anticipation inhaled with a breath.

My Life Within a Frame

They stand there
Sentinels to life
My life
Framed in gold and silver
Snatching from tidbits of time
A family museum with me as a guide
Roaming the halls of memories
How easy to look and touch a frozen moment
To smile
To remember
To feel the inner reassurance that once was
Is still there----somewhere
Bringing forth new memories
To be placed alongside as

My life within a frame.

Summer Solstice

The golden bursts from the sun illuminate all objects
Tinting the world in a rainbow hue of brilliance
The undulating waves of heat rise from the earth's surface
Nature's way to encase and hold hostage to the sun those who tread
    upon the earth
Nurturing the seeds of life giving sustenance
The mirages of tenuous currents of air
Float over the baked furrows of the unproductive earth
The tears of heat flow freely from the porous membranes of humankind
The sun unrelenting in its power to promise both growth and
    destruction
A glorious orb upon which life is suspended
Eternally centered in our universe.

Shadowy Mists

Mists emerge from the crevices of life
Forming an eerie backdrop of greyness
Images sway and disappear into the harvest nest of shadowy souls
I pass on and feel the presences of others
My body a phantasm image of an undulating unknown
The manifest dimensions of life emanate around me
My hand reaches forward
It is there but yet gone
I seek the place where I am drawn
Senses echo the spirals of breathing entities
I see but can't reason
Knowing who is there a vapor away
Swirling sensual mists of doubt tease the mind and the place where I have to search
Flailing figures disappear through the dimensional mists of lives and history
There is no shape nor substance to the whole of me or of the one I seek
The bodies dissemble
Leaving me broken
Continuing to search to find and touch as the I of me decomposes into the prevalent greyness
Then emerge once again from the annals of specters
My silent footfalls on the unoccupied ashen world.

Life's Purpose

During the seasons of our lives, we travel down many diverse roads. Every path that we take, places a different mantle which rests upon our shoulders. These roles offer us an opportunity to utilize various skills and fulfill that human need to be wanted and, perhaps most of all, to have a purposeful identity.

As the years meld one into the other, we shed many of our identities and take on new ones. Now, for many of us, the challenge of finding, once again, a new path through the multiplicities of life can become troublesome. We are no longer needed in many of our previous capacities because our lives have advanced to a different place on an untraveled path.

We may often ask, "Who am I?" or "What do I do know?" That which we were once valued for is now no longer a prominent aspect of our persona. Yet, the desire to be needed, to be part of something, to once again have a specific identity and be capable of procuring a new path can be overwhelming.

Individual value is a very personal insight. Our talents, desires, emotions, and intellectual needs take us to a multitude of possibilities but finding that specific highway to walk on that will fulfill those needs and empty spaces that are now there can be daunting. As life often dictates, we find ourselves making decisions that lead to some level of personal fulfillment. We place a new mantle upon our shoulders, some we may discard, but others rest gently, and we, once again, find that we are needed and wanted.

The Endless Prescription Saga

I have become the mirror image of my parents. For many years, my sister and I ordered and counted out in individual Ziploc bags our parents daily medicinal necessities. Many years have passed since then, and subsequently I found myself doing the identical procedure for my husband and myself. As our medical needs constantly changed, this procedure became more challenging.

Now, I start off each day taking out my little bag of pills that I had previously filled and my morning glass of juice. Did I ever envision that I would need so many prescription medications? No, that was for my parents and old people. How did this happen to me?

Well, it appears that the human body malfunctions when you least expect it to and then you take a pill to help you to function with the malfunction. But, does everything have to stop working at the same time! Now, that I more fully comprehend the aging process, must it be so evident? Perhaps medications should be manufactured to look like the body part they are supposedly helping. Alas, pills come in all shapes, sizes, doses and colors. My little bag of pills is a small rainbow of pharmaceuticals. This, of course, does not include many other vitamins and supplements that reside happily in their bottles.

More problems arise when prescriptions have to be refilled or renewed. Some prescriptions require an immediate ride to the pharmacy; others can be ordered by phone or online, and some cannot be refilled or renewed until a certain date that is proudly displayed on the bottle. Therefore, we not only have become walking medicine cabinets, but we are walking and talking calendars chained to our prescription needs and their dates.

Life does have its mountains and valleys, and this dilemma is just part of the process. Perhaps, someone will come along with an app that can take over all the necessities and nuances of this medication task and just leave us with our daily doses neatly lined up on the kitchen counter waiting for us to start each day. That would be the beginning of a new era in medical history.

Point of View - Great Expectations

Youth brings with it the limitless quest of possibilities. Seeking all those pathways to fulfillment that dreams lead us down. Some pursuits are reached; others are abandoned, and life and its responsibilities settle into a formula for survival. No one is left untouched by the pitfalls and the lofty highs of experience. The old adage that experience and maturity are the colleges of knowledge comes to fruition. We learn and adapt in many ways, and some occurrences we never thought would come our way ultimately do. The times that are a feast of happiness leave us content and always wanting more.

At some point, we know that it is time to retreat or hang-up our hats and find "a place in the sun." This quest is more than Don Quixote and his windmill. It is a time to find, perhaps develop, and expand upon the foundations we have already built over many productive years. A new identity is wrapped around the old one, and the blending of the two commences. We make of our opportunities what we choose to do with them. Great expectations are not limited to a specific age group or based solely on experience or education. They are within our power and only determined by our own willingness to experiment and broaden the base line of life that each one has built upon.

Fulfillment and contentment can be found in the smallest of achievements. Success brings with it a willingness to try again in any direction. Failure is just a stepping-stone to the next attempt. Each day is what we choose to do with it, and each day can have great expectations,

Point of View – Friendship

Amid all the species there is one constant. It is the need for contact with another of the same ilk. Whether it is a herd, gaggle, flock, club or a team, the overwhelming instinct is to find common interests with another. Humans navigate the ocean of people to find a safe harbor where one is comfortable and accepted as an equal. There are no hard and fast rules in this maneuver, but it is how we function. There is that fundamental requisite to belong, to have a family and friends, and to explore the many opportunities that are given in return.

Friendship is the motivation that has little girls playing together with their dolls and boys with their trains and cars. Maturity may and does alter the common ground, but the need and desire is always there. A friend is a phone call away. A friend is there through the ups and downs of life, and, in return, you have become a friend. The mutuality of this experience is a shield against the bangs and bruises that often accompany life's living.

"No man is an island," is so very true. The human spirit craves human social contact. The touch of one hand to another or a hug for reassurance alters the daily disillusions we all face. Friendship builds trust, confidence, love and the emotional needs that are human. The laughter of people, the delight in the voice and face of a person when you meet, and they see the same response in you is what it is all about. The ability to give of oneself unselfishly is the foundation for friendship and the magic of understanding each other without uttering a sound.

We use voice tones, facial expressions and body language to project our intentions. It is so much more fruitful for all those concerned when we willingly open our hearts and just let someone in.

Lydia Bargiuk

"No man is an island" by John Donne

The Present Moment

Lithe, shadowy trees…tall, stalwart pines…
summer woods.
I enter the inviting coolness.

Chandeliers of muted light…
The sky above, a dome of blue...
a filigree of green.

I travel in the turning and twisting greenness.
Suddenly, the path diverges.
Which should I take?
Like Robert Frost, the one less traveled on?
Or the well-beaten path that most have done?

I pause… Nearby, I hear a stream gushing, gurgling…
nestling in fluorescent greens, dusky browns.
Sun-gilded grasses lace its banks.
A light breeze ruffles overhanging limbs.

It glides and swirls in reverberating melodies.
Waters froth in the jeweled sunlight.
Further down below, a trickle…
Calm…peaceful…enveloping…

The pulsing notes of silence…
an occasional song of a bird
or the rustling of leaves…

The magic of the present moment…
Refreshed and resolute…
I continue on my way…

The I….The Me

The human condition…
Its pathos…its nobility…its ignominy…
It straddles two distinct worlds:
The world of the I…the world of the Me.

The I and the Me…residing side by side,
Sometimes in harmony…at times, in strife.
Like two sides of a coin, they are inseparable…
Yet two disparate sides of the human condition.

The outward I…boastful, cruel, cold, indifferent…
thrust into the world to hurt, to deceive, to maim.
And the Me…the gentle touch, the loving embrace…
Soft, caring, courageous…
Conceived in humility…
Nurtured in beauty…in truth…

Oh! How wonderful the world would be
if there was more of the gentle, the kind, the loving Me!

Droplets of Time

youth…
a constant noon…
idyllic…joyous…wondrous…

slowly shadows creep in…
eventually twilight
makes its stealthy appearance…

and memories,
like droplets of time,
wash over our present and future…

In Defense of Winter

winter…our maligned season…
we speak of your icy fingers.
we call you Old Man Winter.
we treat you as an unwanted guest.
yet you possess a quiet charm…
a noble serenity…and also
moments of pure joy.

the cadence of snow falling…whirling…
twirling…a lone deer standing in
naked silence…in billowy whiteness…
an orange marmalade sunset…melting…
petering…into a white horizon…
an early dusk…embracing…cuddling…

indoors…a fireplace blazes…
sparks flicker and fall…
warmth climbs onto my shoulders—
my hands--my face--
pulling me into a world of fantasy…magic…
I hear a whisper…
it is my heart murmuring with pleasure…contentment.

Memories of Christmases Past

dreamingly…I pick up a musical figurine…
a snowman, his hand cupping a red cardinal…
I turn the stem and strains of
I wish you a Merry Christmas
and a Happy New Year
resonate…tingle in the air…

memories of Christmases past assail my senses…
my grandmother…my mother
cooking…baking…decorating…
beautifully wrapped packages nestling
under boughs bathed in multi-colored lights…

caroling…treading from house to house….
the frosty air…and that glorious snow…
fanciful…bewitching…
hot-chocolate…cookies lovingly sculpted…
sprinkled with colored sugar…

if only I could recreate myself as a child…
starry-eyed…bursting with joy and anticipation…
if only yesterdays were again todays…
if only I could recapture the feeling of pure magic…

Friendship

I've known you for many years
and sometimes I wonder
how it all began…
And no matter how hard I try
I cannot recall the exact moment
or place…
Outside the realm of consciousness,
We bonded
and the embryo of our friendship
was formed.
And it grew---continues to grow---sustained and
nourished by moments of
shared time and space…
And also by shared vicarious experiences
when you listen and listen in
ruminated thought…
And like the blood that courses throughout
our bodies. . . the flow of mutual love and
caring keeps our friendship gloriously alive…

That Restless Feeling

the shackles of winter…
bruising…continuous…unrelenting…
my thoughts frozen in mid-stream…
I feel nothing.
I imagine nothing.
spring…wrench away winter's onerous grasp
and arouse your harbingers
from their lingering slumber.
I want to feel alive…truly alive…
to smell the loamy…re-awakening earth…
to hear birds in song…
the rushing of thawing streams…
to see the dusky mauve of crocuses--
the lemon gold of forsythia--
the pink blush of cherry blossoms.
I lift up my head to the endless sky.
Yes…there is a fragrance in the air…
the scent of wellness…joy…
promise…
and an endless array of possibilities…

You Know Me

my inner life…my unique spark of fire…propelling…
mine "to be"…

I never realized how much you really know me…
      my little passions…things that sustain me…
      things that color my life…

oh! how much you understand me…cultivating…
  complementing your needs with mine…
our interplay of needs…touching…harmonizing…

in the winter…
there are the trips to the MET…
    I walk from painting to painting…
        immersing myself in the composition…
          in the colors…ingesting the artistry of the painter…
            the old masters---the impressionists---the moderns…
    you sit quietly on a bench…imbibing the ambience
    of the room…
    attentive…contemplating…

in the spring and fall…
we stroll along woodland paths…in fields of wild flowers…
  in luscious, sculpted gardens…
nature's splendor on display…the ever-changing canvases…
breath-taking…
alive…

my life…your life…our individual rhythms of life
      sustaining. . .
            unique. . .
                  yet embracing. . .

A Little Romance

idyllic moments from the past…
      we filter out all the mundane…the trivial…the dull…
and what is left is pure magic…little joyful scenes…
      small pleasurable gems…
yes---we are all romantics at heart.
      Reminiscing. . .

a picnic in a shaded wood…
   crispy, savory sandwiches…
     a home-made blueberry pie…
      a book of poems…

a walk along the seashore
   on a cloudless summer day…
     the ocean radiant in blueness…
      waves…frolicking…laughing…

a star-studded sky…
    the night…velvety…caressing…
      soft music pulsing…
      chiffon shimmering in the moonlight…
   and that quivering feeling…
      your gentle look---your loving touch…

Spring in New York

a Sunday morning in April…
sleek skyscrapers…grandiose baroques…
hold up the blue canopy of the sky…

New York cocooned in peace…harmony…
The city, stressed out from the week's
activities, reposes in a well-deserved rest…

ribbons of light gild rooftops…cornices…
splaying on streets…avenues…
a few passers-by sprinkle the side-walks…

strolling contently…
I imbibe the uniqueness of Manhattan…
its charm…its charisma…its diversity...

a gentle pulse permeates the lilting quietude…
a soft breeze caresses my check
with whispers of joy…solace…

Nearby I espy a French café…
the aroma of freshly baked bread…
just-brewed coffee…

entices me to venture inside…
I order a croissant…a cup of coffee…
pensive…musing…I watch the passers-by…

what are they feeling?
a subdued, yet vibrant New York?
a quivering undertone of excitement?

or a link to our common humanity?
all week long…they have been
fighting their way through life…

but now it's Sunday…
and life seems somewhat different…
somewhat better…brighter…

it seems as if the city
has cast off its harried pace…
and assumed an aura of tranquility…

the joy of being alive…
being with family…with friends…
if only for just one day…

Gold

It seems as if was just yesterday.
    soft air…sunshine shafting through the
    scarlet canopy of trees…
a perfect autumn day.

walking in a medley of contentment…
  I turn and see gold.
    Helene…sunlight rippling in her eyes…
      In her smile…
        her greeting effusive…undeterred by time…
          her little dog—silvery--with bows of lavender--
            yapping at her feet.

now I stand beneath the leafless trees…
    the air is cold--a brilliant sun—
    but there is no gold.

Phil de Anguera

Eternity is here

Is gone

Is coming.

Taste the water

as you drink it.

A New Life

Glinting Sunlight,
eye squints open,
OMG..the alarm!
I'll be late!
Tears of shocking relief
press up.

I Retired Friday!

And so it began. Hours stretched into weeks and months with little to do but suggest to my wife how she could better manage our house. Before a year was out, we both realized that we needed a new environment. She saw an Ad. in the Real Estate section about 'Active Adult Communities'.

Having little else to do, we took a drive to investigate. What a confusion: old ones, new ones, golf courses, tennis courts. 'Sounded exhausting. However, when we arrived at this growing community full of trees and a big club house, we started looking at the models in earnest. No grass to mow, no snow to shovel and an actual gated entry. Just think, the security of a gated entry keeping us safe with all the other inmates. Classy!

So, we didn't know anyone who lived here, who was left where we were living? Forget all the exhaustion of moving as it will be the last one with furniture.

That first morning was so quiet; we went to the clubhouse looking for some of that 'activity'. Judging from the crammed bulletin boards, there was plenty to do. Coming across a notice signed by, 'The Trustees' I asked an aging passing resident how one became a Trustee. "See the Warden" says he ambling on down the hall. So many clubs, so little time; surely I will find enough to do to relieve me of having to show my wife how to run our new home.

May the existing God forgive me but I have grown to hate Christmastime.

Persistently repetitive music which used to thrill me with its ancient magic,
now enters a vacant room making it all the more empty by its presence.

The iconic humble gifts of the Magi have lost their spiritual meaning in the stampeding roar of Commerce which has become The Spirit of Christmastime.

The Spirit of Giving, being universal to all truly religious peoples,
should not be taken hostage by secular commerce.

Those sweet Christmases of my childhood thrived on Family togetherness.
Gifts were a sharing of mutual Love further bonding each of us together.

These memories continue to glow,
bringing back Life
to those loves
long gone from this earth.

Each of Us

Has a Story to Tell
That Smiles and Cries
and
Wonders Why:

The emptiness of Anger
The vacuum of Revenge;

The Fear and the Longing

For the Fullness

of Love

Circles

None of us can ever be perfectly still. Aside from our internal bodily functions, we are moving in many directions and distances at the same time. The Earth is moving us around while it is moving around the Sun which, in turn, is following its spiral around the Milky Way galaxy which, itself, continues on its expanding path away from the center of the first creative explosion. That makes five constant compound motions for everything on the surface of the Earth.

Each individual life carries with it a similar compound of influences starting with our unique gene combination which becomes held by an emotional gravity to parents who, in turn, move in the circles of their tribe already moving within its cultural galaxy that is being moved ever so slowly by expanding humanity.

While each of us is a world unto ourselves, we did not come spontaneously into being nor do we continue to exist without a multitude of ties to our ancestral parentage. Honest Humility recognizes and accepts our Being within Beings. Fighting and denying our interdependence to assert an individual superiority leads to the ultimate violence spawned from ignorance into Fear. Understanding and accepting our mutual equality of being generates the empathies of caring and kindness critical to the continuing survival of humankind. Our fragile little temporary worlds need each other like the strands of a web.

Cycles

Floating alone

an open sea;

one horizon

circles around.

Awake alone

quiet night

one awareness

surrounds.

What price wisdom

Tuition of age

Earned in time

Lost to eternity.

The sun comes up

The sun goes down;

The earth keeps goin'

round and round.

Carousel of life,

grab at the rings,

Ride that little horsey;

Get off at the end.

Awakening

As Winter evening darkens

and Day fades to its ending,

the Morning of my Life

Takes on a new beginning.

Knowledge

Quietly but reluctantly
Winter's white flakes
relinquish the sky to
rainbow petals of Spring
bursting forth in celebration of
the remarriage of Sun and rain.

Ever anew the mystery
of Life
shrugs off the chill
of Death
reminding us that
our prided banks of Knowledge
rest on
Nothing.

Love

Love sits atop an Olympic mount of
supporting emotions, theories and actions;
its definition, virtually infinite;
its limitations, human;
its attainment, the stuff dreams are built on and poets embrace.

This mount of love,
surrounded by the Plains of Loneliness
pitted with quicksand's of hate,
is lit by
the rainbow of hope.

"Let there be light!"

All I wanted was a floor lamp with multiple heads to further brighten my wife's living area which her macular degeneration darkens every day.

Choosing a local supply store, I found a lamp on display in the lighting aisle with 5 heads on flexible stems. 'Just the thing! The price tag even listed a sale price reduction from $39 to $29. All well and good except that there was not a boxed one anywhere to be found in the surrounding stacks. The only sales person in sight was busy with another customer further advising me, when I asked, that this was not his area. Wandering out into the main aisle along the checkout registers, I spotted a store uniformed man doing nothing.
"Pardon me, Sir, could you please help me find a lamp in stock that I want to buy?"
Well, I'm just a cashier, but I'll see what I can do."
Following me back to my newly discovered display lamp, he started checking the inventory on a little wireless device.
"We have three of them."
At which point, both of us started methodically searching every box label in the entire aisle. No Luck!
He suggested, "Let me have your phone number and I will have the Lighting Manager call you when he returns."
Impatiently, I glanced down at a label with the wrong stock number but a picture remarkably similar to the display I wanted.
"What about this one?"
"That one has brightly colored shades."
"I don't care what color the shades are!"
He pulled the box out. As we started back to the checkout counter, I mentioned that all I really needed was a lamp that would provide as much light as possible for my wife who is slowly losing her sight to macular degeneration.
"I quite understand because I need to use a 300 watt lamp to read late at night.

My doctor asked what I was reading 'till 4 in the morning and I told him, 'The Bible'"

When I quickly glanced over at him, he said, "I am a Priest".

"Sorry, but I just now noticed your collar above your uniform."

He was a slender man in his early forties with slightly unkempt reddish hair and full, kindly, hazel eyes.

"I am working directly with people as Jesus taught us to do."

"You have a lot in common with the Pope."

"I spent 12 years in a Jesuit school."

"Are you...?"

"No.." - a sort of wry smile -

Holding out my hand, "I'm Phil."

Warmly extending his, "I am Father Bill."

As he personally rang me out, he said, "This lamp has been further reduced to $19.95."

Somehow, a strange tingle swept over me.

Looking him full in his eyes, I said,

"Hopefully, we will meet again, Father Bill."

"Surely, Phil."

Father Bill's Faith saturated his presence with a quiet Aura stronger than any human armor.

My Wife was thrilled with the brightly colored lamp shades.

Love in a Bottle

The cherished vintage of long shared love
can only be savored
by those who have lived it.

As the grapes of passion
slowly ferment,
an indefinable delicacy of strength
suffuses these spirits
until both
are one.

When this wine of lives
pours forth
into eternity,
it simply
changes vessels.

Now

Today is
  Today
    Is
    Today,

Winking into
  Afternoon
    'til
Night
  Slowly sleeps into
Tomorrow
   Into
    Today.

Eternity is Here
    is Gone
      is Coming.

Taste the Water
   as you drink It.

Over the years,

as you and your loved one
grow together
in soul and spirit,
their pain
becomes your pain
hurting you all the worse
without the power
to sooth theirs.
The anguish of helplessness
grips your heart
squeezing tears
from the depths of your being.

Reflection on Self

Who am I? Perhaps, what am I?
A flickering spec of sun, water and earth? A complex lump of moving particles brought into being a-top a pyramid of other lumps, destined to support the next on into mysterious Time?

How does this lump become a 'me', a 'who'? What is a 'who'?
"Cogito Ergo Sum", 'I think, therefore I am' stated Descartes.
Who I am requires thought to organize emotions for survival forged through the ages.

Look deeply into your mirrored eyes sans familiar features. You are there. Keep looking. Do you let yourself in or glaze over in fear of revelation? That moat around your castle of self is to keep others at bay.

As completely unique as each of us is, we cannot ever fully know who we are. Looking inward is pursuing the other side of a möbius strip.

The Brutal Logic of our Democratic System

People do not make laws; money makes laws.

People elect representatives, the cost of whose elections paid for by the money and power to control the representative.

Money buys votes through fear planted in ignorance and fertilized by accusations.

Money is greed feeding itself. The larger the money the larger the appetite.
Money unites in corporations controlled by inbred leaderships whose goals are to gain the most money.

The power of the right rides on those who know they are absolutely right and, all who neither agree with nor understand them, are wrong.

The power of the open minded is scattered into insignificance.

These haves only grasp for more, caring little for have-nots be it money or ethics.

Compassionate Reflections

Loneliness is an opportunity,
not a confinement to our past which is but a long shadow.
It is an open door to creative choices and challenges.

Our five senses
Our mind
Our 'Heart'

The many creative arts of music, graphics, crafts, cooking and countless more.

Write your thoughts, if only for yourself;
Written words can be ladder steps to new horizons.

Create a better body to energize your spirits.

Welcome your God into your heart and mind,
filling your spirits' empty rooms with kindness, compassion
and the warming humility
of a loving faith.

My Reflections on Reality

Primal meaning,
Root of truth
commonly drowned
in oceans of words.

We live to survive
from moment to moment,
the horizon of death
beyond our sense.

The final predator,
We hunt ourselves
killing less
than we bear;
suffocating,
ultimately,
this sweet globe
in human waste.

Three dimensional environment
two dimensional life
one dimensional talk

Aches of life
sharpen with age
fish hooks of love
caught deep in your heart
strung on memories
pulled tighter by time
plucked hard by regrets;
'til cut free at last
by that final knife.

So, sing a song
of pain and tears
but remember love
for all those years.

Snippets from the Past

Chill clear August dawn
Geese in rigid silhouette
Corn field being gleaned.

Learning down this open road
Conscious of more than the middle line
Passing some
While being passed
Wondering why we hurry so.

The investment in Friendship
is Love;
with interest payable
in kindness and concern.

Sentiment
is a branch
on the Tree of Love;
never
to be pruned
by reason.

Time smiles at us
with an aging grimace
And we smile back
seeking Solace.

Age and Wisdom
Are Strangers
in their own Land.
While Wisdom ages,
Age acquires no Wisdom.

As these Minutes
Become ever more precious,
even Time to Dream
is rationed.

Dreams mix
Hearts collide
Lives spin
Searching
For a Sun.

Our Spirits
        are Wild Birds
Thrust into
        inherited cages
by a playful God
        of Random Equity.

Pressures-
Weight-
Hard to Breathe;
Suffocating-
Terrifying-
Fight to Live!

Growing up
or
Growing old
Its all the same.
Mind and Spirit
Struggle
To
Push each Day
Aside.

Do You Know

Do you know
why you hurry so?
Is it part of your journey
or, part of your stay?
Is your burden
forgiven,
Your path
free of stones?
Is daylight
still with you,
the darkness,
ahead?
Walk slowly
with love
'til
the end.

Our Fairways Adult Community in Winter   (A study in sarcasm)

Ah… - Bliss. As I gaze out my drafty window into the horizontal snow, this friendly winter scene takes me back to childhood, riding to school though snow on my horse, Happy, one of the meanest animals ever put under a boy. Little did I know that going out of that farm gate would lead, finally, to the Fairways gate. Living hasn't changed all that much, though.

Swimming hole to heated pool; spiteful horse to costly car; mini-tax to taxing burden; farm raised food to mystery meat; sleighs to snow plows...ever onward and upward. Franklin stoves and oil lamps to utility bills.

What a wonderful time it was to be so independent of others and, especially, of Government. Water from a well, fuel from a wood-lot. We have progressed from hard work to obesity and travel expenses.

Illness was simple. If your Dr., who came to your home, couldn't help, your Family did their best for you 'till the end.

Just think, no expensive medicines, hospitals, procedures or specialists to drain your meager worth. Government provided very little and cost very little. People lived and died on their own. Two cheers for Creationism!

Those chintzy Politicians are so right. Everybody can't expect to be kept alive by the rest of us. It costs too much. Let people suffer and die on their own like they used to; or, they could join the Army or, go to prison where there is free health care.

Money is buying our country, anyway, so our children might just as well start getting used to a third world existence of moneyed masters and the invisible gates of financial slavery where life is winter all year.

Ten Years

Ten years in an adult community and
Silence can be

Deafening;

Loneliness,

Suffocating.

Stepping into an early morning,

The voices of children

Tinkling in the wind

Like chimes of
Sunshine

Awakening memories

Lost in the fog of
                        Time.

Nursing Hell

At the end of the hall was a small desk supporting a new book for the reading pleasure of those in the home who could get to it.

The Title: "The Last Days."

How bleeding appropriate! Was it placed there out of sheer stupidity, sick humor or absolute cruelty?

>Where is my little bear – I need it to hold tight. Where did all the love go?
>Far off voices in the hall. No one to talk with nothing to do or plan to do or hope for.
>Wake up – take pills – go to sleep – wake up – eat –
>take pills by the clock but not when I hurt.

>Visitor: "How are you, dear? You are looking better every day. Good by."

>All of those years,
>all of those joys and tears,
>gone
>into nothingness.

>To sleep and to wake,
>to sleep and not to wake.

The Last Bird

The road ahead was long and straight with only mountains a day ahead rising through the gray dust. My daddy was driving very fast after having stopped by our home. He had both of us wearing masks over our nose and mouth to keep out the dust.

"Daddy, why was Mommie sleeping on our carpet?"

"She was tired and it was too late."

"Why were people sleeping on sidewalks and, why were all of the cars parked in the middle of the streets?"

"It was too late."

The stop lights weren't on, either.

I napped from time to time and, when I told Daddy that I had to pee, he stopped in the middle of the road and had me just get out of the car and go on the road.

There weren't any other cars except some stopped in the road along the way.

When I woke the last time, we had already started up a mountain and the dust was sort of thinning out. When we got to the top, we could see the sun and all of the gray dust covered everything for as far as we could see, just like an ocean.

Daddy sat on some rocks and held me on his lap after taking our masks off. We just sat there and looked out while tears crept down his cheeks. "Why are you crying, Daddy?" He just hugged me hard.

In the distance, we saw a bird flying towards us and, finally, landing at our feet. It looked like it had almost fallen from being tired.

The three of us sat quietly together watching the gray dust slowly come further up the mountain till it reached our feet and kept on coming. The bird disappeared into it.

As it reached me, I had a drowning feeling as I breathed in this dust of HATE.

The Empty Room

Walking through the doorway, I entered what appeared to be a normal sized family room. Beautifully framed art work dressed the walls. Centered in the room a long table bore expensive china filled with appetizing finger morsels.

Moving about this room, grateful for the invitation, I began to wonder why. Having inspected the paintings and nibbled some foods, I wandered back over to the door.

There were voices in the room,

none addressed me;

there were eyes in the room;

none looked my way;

so I left
        the empty room.

Marygene Coleman Fagan

Through life's joys, sorrows, adventures, and significant moments, writing poetry has been my stalwart and compassionate companion.

It is the vehicle through which I express my fierce love of family, the sadness of loss, or the exhilaration at nature's wonders.
It is a gift I treasure.

Eternal Tableau

The rains are late.
The animals puzzled.
Dust dervishes swirl above,
the Serengeti floor.
All afternoon, we watch.
The zebras mill about
waiting.
Young striped colts
bend into mothers' side.
At nearly dusk, a stirring,
it is a signal.
Four male zebras step forward.
The wildebeests follow silently,
single-file.

One by one, the line swells.
Sentinel zebra guard the margins.
Close by, a sleek cheetah watches,
green eyes slit, biding her time,
waiting for the weakest,
the straggler,
the infirm.
No need for hurry,
the menu is vast.
Violet, pink and golden bands,
stripe the sky.
We stare in awe at this centuries old spectacle.
The great migration has begun.

Life on the Serengeti

Here on the Serengeti Plain
birth and death,
a constant rhythm
in the pulse of life.

This morning, a zebra mother
gives birth in silence.
The young colt,
struggles to his feet,
warm placenta that gave him life
within his mother, still attached.

Wobbly, he rests against her,
as she lobs her tongue over his
still frail body.
When that first bathing is complete,
other members come to
greet him into the herd.

Now he must gain strength,
for challenges soon loom ahead.
Close by, a lioness finishes her meal –
a zebra caught unawares,
just a striped bit of flesh remains.

Fresh blood lingers,
across her face.
Now her giant paws
swipe away the traces,
and then she sleeps.

Her hunger quenched,
purring,
she slumbers.
Life on the Serengeti beats on.

Reconciliation

Your haunting call to prayer
wakened me each morning.
A reminder that I was in your world
and should hasten my own meditation.
Your women clothed with covered heads and toes,
some bearing burkas with only slits for sight.

Strange to western eyes
you surprised me by your welcome.
Amused me too as the ancient weathered man
admired my made up face.
You wear the powder, you said, stroking your long beard.
I wish our women could
And the plump smiling waiter inquiring if I were Muslim,
at my order of iced tea.
Anshala, he nodded.

I sat in silence thinking,
you must know that people in my country view you with suspicion.
It is true.
Some of your people slew thousands of our citizens,
crushed our buildings, and still boldly plan to do us harm.
We cannot forget that horror, and to forgive,
well, that is questionable at best.

But there are those who respect a higher power
and value the brotherhood of man,
who understand that violence in the name of god is vile.
Although history speaks of gulfs that separate us,
there are those who recognize that all great prophets,
be they Buddha, Mohammed, Christ or Moses urged us to peace and love.

For myself,
I shall recall your morning song and pray
to someday sing together.

Zanzibar Sunset

We sit with outstretched legs,
and sun-scorched arms
The wooden dhow slips silently,
through the Indian sea.

Ebony muscled men wrestle
the half-moon sail.
We watch.
A few hours past, we shrank
this burning torch.

But now it settles in the west,
a giant orb of orange brilliance,
a flame.
We hold our breath and wish
to capture such a moment,
It is not to be.

As it has for time eternal,
the sun sinks into the sea,
leaving only remnants,
of pink and golden ribbons,
in its wake.

Grand Girls

Sweet princesses in pink and purple,
sequined shoes,
small mimes of one another.
We play,
we are a cheetah family,
young ladies sharing tea.
A dollhouse, crafted by my father,
now passed to a new generation.
One, the entertainer,
runner, reader, artist,
a beauty at age seven.
The other,
no less beautiful,
and tender,
She cuddles as I sing her song,
begs me to play "cheetah,"
chats by phone.
Her hugs embrace me in joy.
each a small wonder,
of God's creation.
These girls,
these gifts,
these granddaughters,
that I so love.

The Making of a Man

Boys shouting in Swahili,
dive into an azure sea.
Fingers pointing, daring new feats.
Who dives highest? Deepest?
Who is a contortionist?
Brings me back, near forty years
to the childhood of my son.
Brian, age four, propelling the pool surface,
        Faster,
        Further,
Emerging in squeals of laughter,
        to try again.
At age fifteen, he learns the rough hard ways
        of lobstermen.
Laboring to pull traps from the depths,
        growing stronger, taller,
        finding a passion for the sea.
Now a man, husband, father,
        but still my son.
        I watch.
        He is powerful,
        graceful in water,
Swimming great lengths,
inspiring himself,
to go beyond.
He takes to the bike.
Tackling mountains,
measuring his worth.
        Climbing,
        coasting,
testing his lungs,
then racing against peers.
And confidence grows
now, to the road.

His greatest challenge,
fresh pain,
Muscles scream
bettering himself.
    Always, always,
    New goals,
    new terrain,
    new fellowship,
and the dream looms.
Training,
progressing,
    evaluating,
    Finally, a Wisconsin September,
    he glides through water by the mile.
    Pushes through fatigue,
    covering kilometers on the bike,
    and then the run,
    a marathon,
    the final test,
    but dream in sight.
Reality,
Now victory!
Throwing his hands to the sky,
in celebration.
He is an ironman!

To my Loved Ones

When I depart this world, please celebrate my life.

Share my lure to Africa, the tales I have told you,

remember my zest for adventure.

To snorkel the Great Barrier Reef,

climb the jungles of Rwanda,

raft the roaring Colorado,

explore the grandeur of America,

and test my body in triathlon.

Do not forget my ardor for the written word

or the poetry written out of love for you.

How I rejoiced to see your faces on Christmas Day.

Walk beside the ocean which humbled me,

granting serenity and peace.

And rather recall a Higher Power that sustained me

Never extinguishing the fire of hope,

And in the words of the country singer,

"Please give faith a chance, and don't forget to dance

Reminiscence 9-11

On that dreadful day ten years ago,
my tears were frozen.
Not so today.
That day I watched our buildings crumble,
steel dissolved in flames.
A nations' loss of innocence.
The blue of that day's sky,
belied the horror descending
on us from above.
"Our lives will never be the same"
My husband said.
A prediction soon fulfilled.
Frantic phone calls, where is my son?
On the train?
The elevator?
Trapped?
Or he is wrapped in the thick fog of dust
chasing ghost-like figures in the street?
And then to hear his voice!
Safe, but angry,
and fearful for the world his first born son
will come to know.
That day my tears were frozen.
Not so today.
I relive the evil that still threatens.
I weep with sorrow,
but also pride and gratitude
for family, faith, and for a nation,
united in love for one another
if only for today.

Terror in the Afternoon

Cracked leather boots stand toe to toe,
Sinking into themselves,
Baking on a diving board,
Under the July sun.
"Darn rascals climbed that fence again,"
The pool man grumbles, swearing at the interlopers,
Gingerly grasping each boot,
Kicking open the chained gate,
And walking away.

Scores of joyful children pour through,
Shouts of 'Marco Polo' ring out.
Racers kick into gear,
Splashing, shouting, jumping,
Ducking unsuspecting friends.
A shy girl of twelve,
Practices diving skills,
Down through the green murk
She pushes far below,
Near-sighted eyes sealed.

Floating fabric touches her hand.
She dares a peek,
A khaki-clad figure waves,
Like ocean seaweed.
She flees to the surface.
Now she sits,
Swinging her legs in shallow water.

Long minutes later,
She stares.
The handsome lifeguard drags a bloated figure,
Past screaming children,
Its mouth sags open,
Wrinkled skin steams under the Kansas sky.
Shriveled bare feet, lifeless and stiff.

The 'rascal' who left boots behind,
Has struck one final time.
Destroying our innocence.
In this small Kansas town,
No child will sleep tonight.

Uninvited Visitor

One year ago today,
death visited.
I did not invite you,
nor did I let you in.
But I could feel your breath,
attempt to crush my weakened lungs.
You broke my limbs
and
tore my flesh,
but I resisted.
You jumbled my brain,
and
chained me to my bed,
but you did not break my spirit.
Today I am a woman,
strong once more.
Fit to lift my grandson,
play a game of 'pig',
test my brain,
and
love my spouse.
Yes, I threw you out,
spat into your face,
and focused on survival.
Challenged my body and my soul,
then,
fell upon my knees,
in gratitude,
and prayer.

Upon reflection

When I was small, Christmas magic was slow to arrive,
but finally scents of pine and peppermint
floated through the house,
rivaling smells of that day's baking.
"Always a real tree,"
Mother and I vowed.

A resolution broken by each of us,
After years of battling prickly needles,
in the carpet or our clothes.
Long before little white lights filled,
gardens, roofs and trees,
Mother abandoned multi-colored lighting.
Labeling them as 'garish'.

She adorned our tree with tiny lights of blue,
bundled fresh greens to garnish every shelf,
every table in every room.
Candles of gold and silver 'sprouted' from
those blankets of green.
Excitement peaked Christmas Eve,
with the opening of gifts.

Waiting for perennial late cousins who arrived,
arms wrapped around unwrapped gifts.
Giggling, they scurried to an empty room,
clothing their naked boxes, then adding them
to mounds of presents spilled haphazardly
beneath the tree.

Last arrival always Uncle Tom.
Cigar in mouth, rosy cheeks puffed
as he struggled up the walk.
"Poor Florence, " My mother would whisper,
"I don't know how she does it."
Forty years and more the ritual repeated
each December.

But with the passing of my parents,
keeping Christmas fell to me.
Most traditions kept, some added,
a potent southern comfort punch
and eggnog Christmas morning.

All too quickly my tenure ended,
the torch passed to the women my sons wed.
One by one traditions disappeared,
grandchildren learn new ways to celebrate.
None better than my own,
but different.

So my mind wanders to Christmas Eves of long ago,
to trees attired in blue, scents of baking pumpkin pies,
pine candles burning,
and the echoes of voices we can no longer hear.
And I smile,
as a single tear slips down my cheek.

John Patrick Gatton

Change a perception and you can change a life.
Poetry and well-told stories offer the possibility
of changing perceptions.

There was a time

when I focused on results,
a time of great concentration,
of self-confidence,
exploring, learning,
advancing.

I reviewed telephone books
for the challenge
of memorizing numbers.

I counted black-eyed salmon
in the Hudson River
simply to accomplish an impossible task,
striving always to become one of the fantastic
achievers in the world.

I have changed -
and now write poetry to create
flawed descriptions of possibilities;
later going out to complete related tasks
with vigor and blemished results;

a man now tired of perfection, obsession,
motivation, and hernias created
in striving for perfection.
———
In poetry workshops
I learn the value
of imperfect descriptions
that blow away the idea of faultlessness
and create idyllic perceptions of life's realities.

I am a happy man
searching each day
for ways to imperfectly describe
those lesser things now cherished
as golden achievements.

We Are the Sages

Part I

We are not the matured, we are maturing.

We are the Sages with gifts of experienced living,
those who have sculpted lessons, decisions,
responsibilities, observations,
and consequences
into wisdom.

In our maturing, we have become Sages.
We have learned and discerned things like -
love, praise,
thanksgiving, noticing,
seeing goodness, listening to *their* stories.

As Sages we have - no boundaries,
no rules, no obligations without consent,
no directives, no imposed routines,
no signals of which path to take.
There are no signs saying don't leap ahead.

Deep-water swimming is allowed.

Sponsoring others is rewarding.
Observing the grace, speed,
purpose, and silence in nature is satisfying.

Excitement comes with reaching out to help.
Absolute truths have diminished,
reality is shaped by experiences of love,
friendship, consequences.

Part II

We are free of the claims of others,
loaded with curiosity, open to learning,
wanderers in the world we explore.
We feel the vibrations of life,
the whisperings of those passed.
We long to be with creation,
created beings, created things,
sensing The Creator.

We have learned to express joy,
to relish the vibrations of touch,
to recognize radiant energy
within a neighbor's caring,
We have learned
to avoid sapping conflict,
the value of forgiveness,
harmony created by a smile,
the importance of sharing wisdom,
remuneration within a youngster's thanksgiving.

In our maturing, we have become Sages.
We are active creators.
We are communicators of -
how to, when to, where to,
and if you, I forgive you,
I enjoy you, I respect you.
We are the broadcasters of happiness in life.
We encourage knowing who we really are.

Part III

We are the teachers of how to read road signs,
the wise navigators in the shifting winds of life,
the captains of altered destinies,
the matrons and patrons of mercy,
the providers caring about the needy.
We are armored by life's trials, softened by love,
redirected by serving others,
knowers of how to win and how to learn from losing.

We are the Sages, those with life's wisdom,
the ones who predict with some accuracy.
We are those who know to -
avoid, interweave, create positive goals.

We steer in catastrophic winds.
We paddle when dog-tired.
We give hugs while half asleep.
We tranquilize with adroit touch.
We reassure with an insightful phrase.
We slam the door on inequality.
We walk safely through emotional storms.
We reach and give a dollar from nearly empty pockets.

We speak of how to -
enjoy life,
mingle academia with experience,
provide responsible and honest leadership,
encourage, create dreams,
visualize success,
be with the Greater Being in spite of our flaws.

Part IV

We are the Elders, now the Sages.
We compel listening through dispensing subtle wisdom.
We are guardians of social justice.
We are guides to evolution for younger generations.
We are the qualified advisers, mentors,
diplomats, thinkers, intellectuals,
the skilled, scholars, mystics,
gurus, wizards of how to.

We are the Sages.
Come, gather 'round for we are parents,
teachers, lovers, family promoters,
those who have learned through exciting living,
those who savor, and those who
foster the evolution of humanity.

Senior Citizens – Whisperers of Wisdom

Senior Citizens have become Sages.
Their needs need to be noted.
Their matured wisdom should be mirrored.
Sages' experienced insights need to linger within
the learning minds of the younger generations.

Sages' tales ought to be retold seven fold.
Their stories need to be spoken persistently,
their quotes should be zealously boasted in public places.
Their subtle reactions to today's behavior
demand to be studied passionately.

Sages' words are collectable.
Their sponsoring intentions must be cultivated.
Their enthusiasms require nourishment from welcoming leaders.

Leaders need to know
what Sages believe,
whom they influence,
the worth of their investigated suggestions,
the effects of their approving touch,
the swaying weight of Sages' well-tested beliefs.
Leaders need to know of the inviting nectar
of even one elder's inner peace.

Sages' spirits need nourishment,
their minds need challenge,
their hearts need recognition.

Leaders must learn of these elder journeyers' needs,
their value in broadcasting good news,
their guidance of the young,
the magnetism of even one Sage's unassuming joy.

Within this understanding,
leaders learn to engage Sages
in transmitting exemplary
historical beliefs
that model
loving congregations,
love of neighbor,
freedom to worship, the created worth of each person.

A Laugh Is a Prayer

Your smile is pleasing to each you greet,

your face lights, you chuckle,
then raise your eyes in surprise.
Your reaction to a fractured perception
showers amusement over observing crowds.

You participate
in migration to and from
standard expectations delete comma
with delight.

You like being with agreeable folks
who giggle, articulate humor
and gift the court jester.

Your relaxed face
creates diversion
to fun-filled subjects
that generate stretching smiles
and bright eyes.

Our delight is in watching your face
as your breath burst forth
and seriousness heads north
to the land of silence.

It is delightful to believe
that your laughter
charms the creator
of you and all that is.

Equality

Being equal, we are just as nature has made us.

Being equal, one must have complete respect for self,
curiosity about the stories of each person,
and happiness when encountering other people.

Being equal, we are a companion for a minute or a lifetime.
Equality exists when each has an equal position in life,
the same justice, the same civil rights,
and respect for the gifts of each person.

Effects of equality include encouragement of other people,
loyalty to all people, respect for the talents and skills of each person,
and equal votes in all important events.

Effects of equality include
the experience of happiness,
free and friendly laughter,
independence, freedom
and mutual support.

These effects of equality exist when
we have mutual respect for each person
without premature judgment,
when we have happiness
in a meeting with other people,
and when we have the desire
to contribute to the life of each person.

We author
equality in this world.
We create
the benefits of equality in this world.
We receive the effects of equality in this world.

Chamber of Unnoticed Voices

Recorded here in this chamber of listening
are the speaking voices
of those who are little noticed.

The pleasurable sounds
they create in this place
stimulate the listener's heart and spirit.

The voices of
a farmhand intoning a Chant,
a mother's soothing timbre,
a monk's quiet tranquilizing voice,

a child singing within happiness,
a traveling man speaking of family,
a shepherd's quieting lyrics,
an eskimo mimicking a polar bear,

an Irishman's rhythmic story,
a beggar's praise of God,
a coach counseling a neighbor's child,
a woman bowed in thanksgiving over a rice bowl.

Each unnoticed voice now speaking,
being heard praising the Creator
in this place of sharing and listening
among equally created beings.

Upside-down Baseball

My director of poetry said,
write upside down.

So I stood on my head,
watching a kid's baseball game.

Seeing only feet,
my view of the game was different.
One set of feet pointed in,
indicating lack of talent.
One set pointed out
stating a suggestive mind set.

When the ball was here,
feet moved to and from.
When the ball was there,
feet stood still.

When the ball was coming,
feet moved towards it.
When the ball was going,
feet seemed relaxed.
When the click of the bat
on the ball was heard,
feet came to attention.

When the crowd roared,
feet were straight
pointing toward the loudest voices.
When enough play was completed,
feet ran towards the dugout.

Then came new feet
with shoes of a different color,
though patterns of movement
were the same.

When I got upright,
I knew I had seen the game
from a new and lesser accepted view.
Several have told me that my view of any game
was never the same as anyone else's.

Upside-down views of life
are seldom accompanied by applause,
except from those who view things differently.
To me, this comment seemed to be a compliment.

Eye Contact – A Grandparent's View

Each of six grandchildren
looks into my eyes
when talking to me,

transmitting these effects and messages –

refreshment of my love for them,
confidence that I am important,
love conveyed to me,
knowledge of their intent,
detection of humor,
understanding of sadness,
insights into current emotions,

vibrancy of her or his personality,
fermentation of my self-confidence,
increase in my mental alertness,

acceptance - they of me and I of them,
observation of human complexities,
love flowing, peacefulness,
confirmation of the value of my listening,

the power of recognition – given or received,
reflection of historical family values
remembered in living cells,
happiness within the family,

the joy of realizing I am loved by two generations
one of whom I have fathered,
one of whom I have nurtured
as a member of a family
dating back to Adam and Eve.

Perhaps someone should soon examine
the effects of texting
while we are visiting with friends.

Springtime in the Mountains

(In thanksgiving for the days spent at "The Mountain.")

Just being among the rough structures,
the fallen trees,
the growing saplings,
the singing winds,
the scent of the animals,
the blueberries,
the dogwood trees,
the quietness,
the bulk of water in the river,
the trout in the fresh water,
the hanging limbs full of new sprouts,
the quietness of the mother deer,
the sound at the beehive,
the density of life,
the effects of the penetrating sun-rays,
the sounds on the lake,
the random patterns,
the history of rebirthing,
the potential of the pinecones,
the absorbing power of the trees,
the vestibule at the forest's opening,
breathing in the life-giving oxygen,
is enough to make my day.

What Is a Friend?

A friend makes me feel good by speaking,
writing, listening,
touching to heal, interceding,
providing direction,
chatting about this and that,
changing my frame of reference,
mentioning my name to someone who might like me,
flashing a light in the darkness,
taking me to a movie,
telling me I am a good guy,
telling me that God is good,
stopping by just to say hi,
baking a cake, smiling when I say hello,
doing me a small favor,
renting a boat for fishing,
lifting the load I can't lift today,
saying hello to my children,
asking about my family,
calling just to tell of good news,
telling me of today's troubling situation,
listening to a clarifying word,
being at the place of community praise for the Greater Being,
telling me I do good stuff,
reminding me of the goodness around me,
taking my child to a game,
standing in a grocery line for an ill neighbor,
cleaning up around the place,
inviting us to share a movie,
visiting a friend in tough times,
contributing to the well-being of those in need,
reminding me of my own clutter,
greeting me in a crowd, being happy,
laughing at a lot of things that seem so burdening,
broadening my responses to life events,
reminding me that people are God's children…not mine.

A friend does all of these things and more while expecting
and appreciating the same from me.

Friends seem to make my world-go-round.
And, I for them.
Maybe that is why we easily call each other when
the world is in sync, and when it is not.

Woman of the 1940s

Mom stood at the electric range,
dropping into the pressure cooker
a piece of roast beef.

A neighbor sold her the used cooker
that would save her an hour
of cooking time each day.

The kitchen was small
accommodating only two for coffee.
In the sitting room was a floor grate
that allowed the warm air
from the basement coal burning furnace
to percolate its way up through the house
to the second floor.

At the back of the yard
was an ice house that contained
300 pound ice blocks stored for future
distribution, either at the street's curbing
or on the route that Dad drove
while carrying ice to the town people.

Mom had given birth to five
healthy children
while the effects of the Great Depression
still held on with its grip of misery.

The house stood two blocks
from the Square,
and only 300 steps from the church.

The youngest child would come in
to complain about being bullied
by big brother who scared him
with images of ghosts, Frankenstein,
and the Wolf Man.
Mom had heard it all before and knew
how to comfort the little fellow.

It was the desperation of so many people
suffering from the lack of life's basics
that bothered her.
The economy was dark.
The depression was real.
She and Dad had learned to live
with these depressing factors
while nurturing more children
than common sense would say is possible.

I often wondered what motivated parents
with five growing, always hungry children to be
determined to nurture love and happiness
within such tough times.

Charlie's Story

My friend Charlie and his wife recently kept two grandchildren, Paul and Cindy overnight, Charlie told me this story about the meaning of their visit in terms of his own family history.

Paul is nine years old, Cindy is four. Charlie and Paul were up early after the first night of the visit. Charlie had his coffee and was cooking eggs for the kids' breakfast. He and Paul were having a conversation about baseball when four-year-old Cindy came into the kitchen looking a bit tired and not so ready for the day. Paul went over to Cindy, gave her a hug, and said, "Good morning Cindy." "Good morning, Paul," the four year old Cindy replied in a rather tired tone.

Then Charlie said to me, "This was one of the most moving moments of my experiences as a father and a grandfather." I thought the hug and the "good morning" were nice gestures, but did not get that the gestures were so significant. Not really getting his point, I asked Charlie, "Why?"

He replied, "When I was a small boy visiting my grandmother, she would greet me in the morning by saying hello and then give me a hug. At home, mom and dad always said good morning and occasionally followed up with a hug. My wife and I always greeted our children with, "Good morning" and when they needed it we gave them a hug. Our daughter and son-in-law greet these two children with a "good morning," every day. Hugs are given whenever they seem to need one." I said, "It sounds like a nice thing to do, but why is it so significant to you?"

My friend Charlie, an ordinary man, then awakened me to a remarkable insight. "Our Faith has brought forth for thousands of years the belief that God is love, and has asked us to love one another. I have just witnessed the fifth generation of my own family living a simple morning-time event based on that belief and the fulfillment of the request made in each generation of us."

He continued, "My grandmother was born circa 1865. My parents were born circa 1890. I was born in the 1930s. My grandmother hugged me when I saw her. Our daughter was born in the 1970s. Her children were born in 2003 and 2008. I have just witnessed the result of believing that love is our source, and that in doing what Love asked us to do we experience happiness. Surely you understand, I am witnessing about events that have occurred in our family during three centuries."

This ordinary man enriched my experience of life and confirmed the value of a positive belief system.

Life Is A Beach

Calmly, he sits in the sand at the water's edge
knowing that under the sea's surface
are currents,
swift currents,
violent currents,
mammals as large as a ship, and
massive grinding continental shelves
creating vibrations that rattle the sea.

The fire exploding sun
lays its burning rays on his naked skin.

Calm he is, for now is the season
of the tranquil winds.

Life Is Random

He bet upon the snowstorm
and found the mountain top covered
with powder for his skiing.

She bet upon the rainfall
and found the river full and swift.

Together, they bet upon history's weather map,
then discovering life forces are unpredictable
and dependent on a nature greater than they.

School of St. Jude - Tanzania, Africa

Yesterday,
3 students,
the poorest children
with the least hope,
were greeted and invited
to become educated.

12 years pass.
Different parents standing in lines
waiting with children,
applying with hope to boost 1 child
into flourishing life experiences.

Charitable contributors achieving
results only a few could imagine.
1800 students, an outcome with saintly elements -
enthusiasm for purpose,
belief that the task can be done.

Dedicated people with limitless
faith-saturated images of success.
Redefining these terms -
fun, fulfilling work, simplicity, and empathy.
Emptying themselves of steadfast opinions
while embracing full respect for each person.

They focus on results,
evolving as attracting centers
of positive energy.
Moving quickly aiding
today's distressed child,

savoring rich images of possibilities
anointing success with love,
learning from failure.
perpetually re-igniting hope.
Letting go, they encourage
free-flowing knowledge.

Living within systemic equality
they provide forward-motion pushes,
guidance to graduation,

each year greeting new families
standing in line and full of hope
to boost 1 child
into flourishing life experiences.

Water

(This poem honors the charitable organization - Change A Life Uganda)

For two days a man searched for water,
his body's cells malfunctioning,
his electrical system closing down.
Instinctively, he intoned a plea for help

his words lingering
as a man and woman stood before him
with pails of pure cold liquid.
Each dipped hands into a pail
cupping water for his sipping,

easy, they said, let your body adjust.
They washed his face,
then his feet.

Thirst builds innate knowledge
that dehydration slows life's energies,
destroys the nervous system.

Only education brings knowledge
of economic effects of a thirsting community
constantly engaged in seeking and transporting water.

In two days of thirst, a community suffers,
faltering and edging into death.
Human attention cauterized to basic survival.

Through gifting tutors, a community learns to tell its story,
to look for that man and woman who know freedom
and possess the blessed resources.

When they meet, hope arises, resources flow,
water is found, equipment purchased,
drilling penetrates the resistances, pipes fill with water,
thirst is eliminated, dreaming begins.

The dream constructers appear, people who build -
teachers, cooks, those who care.
Children flourish as they experience equality,
bringing a new thirsting
satisfied by a dimensionless resource,
existing knowledge freely shared –

developing rules of ethical living, neighborliness,
the flow of love - resulting in evolving culture, health, wellbeing,
and advancement of generations yet to come.

Water is essential
to life
to equality,
to education,
to ethical behavior,
to curiosity,
to generosity,
to the flow of love
through a nourished community.

Those with resources are essential to expansion
of physical, mental, emotional health
and ethical community development.

They are the men and women holding
the pails of cold, abundant water.

To be Mother is to Create

(To Barbara, Mother's Day Note, 2014)

Within mother is the gift of life.
Through mother, life is given, birthed, created
with the great Creator.

Through my mother,
I was given life.
Through my wife,
the lives of our children
are given the same.

From mother
is received her essence,
her happiness, her gifts.
Each person shows affection
simply because she exists.

Within mothering she promotes -
good character,
equality,
persistence,
desire for happiness,
acceptance of free will,

the values
of respecting others,
dignifying, touching, supporting,

forgiving, forward movement,
socializing, stretching,
reaching, accepting,
recognizing, and graduating.

In the practice of mothering,
she moves on, reaches out,
searches anew,
becomes a believer,
transmits love,
magnifies joy,
accepts sorrow,
regains the verve of life.

She stands straight,
trips occasionally,
rebounds, welcomes, strengthens;
laughs at her own mistakes.

I am a credible witness
who has intimately observed
several mothers in their
life-enhancing roles.

One, my mother, I observed
as an infant, a child, an adult.
One, my wife, I observed
as a husband
and the father
of our five children.

To be a mother is to give life.
The practice of mothering creates the verve in life.

Una Nota per il Giorno di Madre, 2014

(A note for mother's day in the Italian language -
respecting friends of the Italian culture)

Essere madre è creare.
La vita è nutrita dalla madre.

Dentro la madre è il regalo della vita.
La madre dà la vita,
poi la nascita.
Lei crea con il grande Creatore.

Mia madre mi ha dato la vita.
Attraverso mia moglie,
la vita per i nostri figli è stati
dato nello stesso modo.

la felicità è ricevuto dalla madre,
con molti i regali da lei.
Ogni persona ha affetto per lei
semplicemente perché lei è.

La madre con esperienza
promuove buon personaggio,
l'uguaglianza,
la persistenza,
il desiderio di felicità,
usare di libero arbitrio,

anche i valori del rispetto degli altri,
abilitando, toccando, il sostegno,
il perdono, il movimento in avanti,
la socializzazione, l'allungamento,
raggiungendo, accettando,
riconoscendo, e laurea.

La madre con esperienza
rilascia, viaggia su, raggiunge,
cerca per idee nuovi,
diventa un credente,
condivide l'amore,
a espande gioia,
accetta la tristezza,
ritrova la verve della vita.

Lei stare dritto in piedi,
inciampa, rivitalizza, accoglie, rafforza;
lei ride ai suoi errori.

Io sono un testimone credibile.
Ho osservato intimamente diverse madri
nei loro ruoli che migliorano la vita.

Una, mia mamma, ho osservato
da bambino, da giovane, da adulto.
Una, mia moglie, ho osservato da marito
e da padre dei nostri cinque figli.

Essere una madre è dare la vita.
La madre crea la verve della vita.

Bee Friendly

To be Bee friendly
a Bee must learn how to dance,
sing, move in concert
with the colony's traditions.

The dance of friendliness
gives proper direction, and distance.
Body moves are in well known gestures
describing scents, tastes, sounds, sights,
how something feels, where it is.

The Bee's song must identify turning points,
sights to see, and turn around markers.
Words are not said, would be misunderstood.
A Bee cannot speak in a commanding voice;
doesn't know how.

To be Bee friendly, one must know
the colony's ways, the dances,
the songs, the description of distance,
the place of life-giving nectar,
the definition of quality, the process
of hunting, retrieving, homing.

One must participate
in colony building
to be Bee friendly.

To be human friendly one must know how to search,
to reach out, to find, to be with, to stand ready,
to display love, to return, to assist, to seek positive views,
to encourage proper turns,
and when to simply rest.

Are these processes so different?
Aren't the results alike?
Don't the Bees buzz around
to keep the colony healthy,
well fed, perpetual?

Don't we share the same purpose
in our sharing community
as the Bees in their buzzing friendliness?

From the Palm of Your Hand

You write passionately about life,
I, your reader, do enjoy it.

My mind echoes with the beautiful sounds
created in the speaking of your words
describing stimulating observations.

Your interpretations of life, action,
and fossils create happiness within me.

Your words ignite mind-filling scenes,
taking me out of tradition,
guiding me to new thoughts;
new ways to perceive and behave.

I am stirred by your explanations
of what you see, your perspective
of what is known,
your thinking about our destinies,
your view of our reactions,
and all that we accomplish.

Suppose the world were occupied
by only you and me -
the only reader considering your views,
your interpretations of life,
your truths.

In this pondering and acceptance,
I predict I would in turn
positively influence
all living entities,
as we are called to do.

Leave It Out

Some things should be left in,
some things left out.

City dwellers should know that organic is good
though not be told that organic means
tomato plants are raised
in sod soaked with cow manure.

Some things should be left in,
some should not.
A manager from Atlanta
promoted to work in New York City
should know it's a nice deal;
though not told of the heat
generated in a stalled subway car
during a simmering summer day.

Some things should be said,
some things should not.
A journey should be sold
as a destination in the mountains.
The half-day bare-back ride on a donkey's back
should be left without description.

War and the Village

We grew up
in a small town, a village,
less than one thousand people
spent the 1940s and 50s,
therein the quietness
doing the chores of the family business,
with welcoming neighbors
who expected a morning greeting.

Travel was limited to a few miles.
Home, a good place to be
with nearby grain fields,
farmers plowing, raking,
harvesting.

WWII caged us in.
We younger ones wondering
why older brothers
and nurses had to go to war,
had to leave the village
to go to battlefields.

What madness
was out there taking
family members into
vicious, bloodletting places?
Even I remember the commonly destructive
nature of Hitler, Tojo, Mussolini.

In 1943 my brother, Don,
became a Navy Pilot flying the lumbering
but effective PBY aircraft while serving with honor.

We often wondered what happened
during those warring years that
precipitated returning veterans'
avoidance of the villages,
returning to the industrialized cities,
working hard for years until tired out
by the inner conflict caused
by horrible, blighting war memories

Thinking more now
in free time
to make sense of life

reflecting on how good it was
in the quiet town,
small village, really.

They were war scarred,
reexamining how life was in that village
with family and friends who didn't travel,
who need a recognizing wave of the hand in the morning,

content to be one of the neighbors
wanting the security of home, a village,
a place of peace and morning hellos.

12 years after my brother,
I became a navy pilot
capable of delivering weapons
of tremendous power
and devastating impact.
I, too, had become a warrior.

Now, it is I who reminisces about that peaceful village
with nurturing neighbors and warm hellos.
Farmers in the fields plowing, raking, harvesting…

To know Fran Karnish

is to experience

how shared love feels
how life is encouraged
how a smile affects a mood
how purpose leads thought
how mother appreciates child
how motivation stirs accomplishments
how accomplishments are beginnings
how encouragement stimulates motivation
why love is important in creating verve
how new beginnings bring hope
how hope thrives in love

I know Fran
In knowing her,
all of these
I have experienced

Elaine Grassi

The task of the poet
is to arrange skillfully the words
that life has spoken to her.

April Has Arrived, My Love

It's April,
that sweetest month when nature is reborn.
Awakened from long winter's frozen slumber,
all life returns to grace our waiting joy:
birds, flowers, trees, the welcome warming sun.

The perfume of the vernal earth enchants me;
profound nostalgia seeps into my soul
and fills my thoughts with memories of our youth.
Ah, now I understand why April
has earned the title, month of poetry.

Together we have walked, my dearest,
through fifty Aprils of the years gone by.
As we reflect upon our lengthy journey,
where, in our lives, is poetry to be found?

A poem must always speak the language
of the soul and also of the heart,
but then grow, take form, be crafted
till its sentiments, in beauty, can be told.
Observe how the artist his pottery creates:
He caresses the clay with his hands
As he makes it grow and take shape
And at last, in the furnace, perfects it.

Again we walk, my dear, through April
although our steadfast steps are slower now.
In retrospect we see how we have grown
and how the potter's hands and wheel have shaped us
and how the kiln's fierce heat has made us strong.

As we approach our final Aprils, we discover
where in our lives our poetry is found:

A poem is a gift of God's design.
I am your poem, my love, and you are mine.

For Ray

(*Written three weeks before he succumbed
to ALS, Lou Gehrig's Disease*)

I stand at the edge of the ocean
toes curled into the wet sand
the spent waves caressing my legs.
I watch you floating a few feet away.
How many years have passed
since you were drawn into these waters!
The tide slowly pulled you
to where you could no longer stand.
I took you in my arms and held you,
my buoyancy keeping you afloat,
treading water endlessly.
We are both tired now
and know the kind and loving act
is to let you go and keep my vigil in the shallows.
The gentle waves carry you toward me.
Reaching out, I lightly touch your hand
before the tide takes you just slightly further
out to sea,
back and forth floating,
in acceptance, not struggling,
knowing that one day--not knowing when--
a great wave will come
and wash you to that vanishing point
where sea meets sky.
The salt of my tears will join
the salt of the ocean
before I turn away and walk once more
upon the dry sand,
a stranger in a once-familiar land.
There will be an emptiness.
Yet there will be a gift
to fill that void.
Yes, there will be a gift
for you,
for me –
Peace.

Fragments

Chancing upon a notebook, decades old,
handwriting from my middle years—
ideas   undeveloped,   left to wither
         on the   yellowed pages,
I see life   composed of
          fragments.
  What once begged for   completion
abandoned   scattered on the   sea
       of forgetfulness
  or left neglected   in the shadows
      of preoccupation—
the garden   planned
    but   never   planted,
  friendships   severed
     by space,   time, the
pressing needs   of the present—
  tableaux   half recalled
    brief   moments from the past—
faces   whose names
     have slipped through
 the tired fingers   of the mind.
What value   to these puzzle pieces
  that   cannot   interlock?
What comfort   in the partial
  never to be whole?

And yet, could these   displaced
      shards
be brought together,
tossed into some cosmic kaleidoscope,
rotated gently by loving hands,
raised to the eyes for kindly viewing,
might not life's fragments
arrange themselves into
a beautiful unique design
as bits of brightly colored glass
united
and brightened by the streaming sun
transform themselves into
a wondrous rose window
worthy to adorn a great cathedral.

It's Not About the Darkness

My younger years, I sensed the waning of the summer
through sight and touch and smell.
Evening after evening, the sunset,
in gradual steps,
brought darkness ever earlier.
The green and rainbow colors of the flora
changed to brilliant orange, gold, then brown;
the leafy trees stripped naked to their bones.
And how many times on a crisp autumn day
have I said, "It smells like fall."?

Strange that only now
my ears perceive the changing of the seasons.
The summer dusk and darkness
held a symphony of nature:
the gentle, sporadic "goodnights" of the birds
as they bedded down for sleep
followed by the raucous serenade
of tree frogs and various night creatures
singing for their mates.

Only now I note
the slow and steady hush of daylight's end.
Darkness tiptoes in, each night more quietly,
Until at last it comes in silent cold.

Should I mourn the dying of my world?
Stepping out into the cool night air,
I stargaze through the clearer autumn sky
and realize
another half the world
sees a different display of stars at night.
On the other side of the equator—
that line that both divides and joins our hemispheres—
the Southern Cross is the guiding beacon,
and on our side, the North Star is our guide.

As my environs fade to dormancy,
that other region greets spring's warmth and life:
the glorious beauty of the fecund earth,
the perfumed fragrance of the trees and flowers,
the joyful chorus of the night.

We are one world.

Quest

Disquieted by my lack of inspiration,
I journeyed forth one radiant spring day
in search of a poem
as if I were a butterfly collector
who arms herself with field glasses and a net
hoping to capture the elusive creature,
bring it home and arrange it
in a pleasing form,
confident it could be found
in one of nature's charming hiding places
from which they had surprised me in the past.

The sight of tiny golden birds
flitting blithely across high treetops
briefly tickled my soul
until they flew away
leaving me to stare
at the empty canvas of the sky.

I stopped a moment to admire
my neighbor's regal irises,
their purple heads perched proudly
on tall stalks of green.
As lovely as they were, it soon was clear
no poem was hiding in this flower patch.

Gazing up at azure skies,
I sought to picture a familiar form
in the slowly-moving fluffy cotton clouds.
No trick of the imagination
could coax the floating white mutating shapes
into any earthly figure.

The laughter of a child who skipped gaily down the street--
her elderly grandparents straining to keep pace—
revived my spirits.
Surely there must be a poem here.
But it was tucked securely in their pockets,
unwilling to be shared with me.
Returning home with empty net,
I found a note taped to my door:

"I rang the bell, then knocked and knocked again.
You were not home, so it was all in vain.
Your hunting trip could only leave you lonely.
Unless I come as gift, you do not own me.
After all these years, I thought you knew
that you do not find me, I find you."

Rhymes on Wrinkles

Sad to say, while growing older,
the marks on my face are growing bolder.
Horizontal lines across my brow
are visible without glasses now.
Amorphous brown spots are clearly seen
where freckles have never ever been.
The experts say—for me too late—
"Here's how your skin can avoid this fate:

"You must stay indoors; eschew the sun.
Don't go outside till day is done.
No squinting at something that's hard to see,
crow's- feet will spread like the chestnut tree.
Don't scrunch your nose when you smell a bad stench,
mustn't purse your lips, so you can't speak French.
You must always preserve a visage bland.
'Relax facial muscles!' is our command.
Drink lots of water, but most of all,
never touch a drop of alcohol.
Don't pout, laugh or smile or frown or cry.
These tasks can be mastered if only you try."

I can tell you that I would never trade
my wrinkles for a life lived in the shade.
Ingesting water is certainly fine
but a gourmet meal just begs for wine.
I've spent my days in sun, fog and rain,
known joy and sorrow, both health and pain.
I've frowned and laughed and smiled and cried
with family and friends though some have died.
So my face is "weathered" as the saying goes,
but "weathered" means "survived" as everyone knows.
My brown spots and wrinkles I shall wear with grace.
Consider them medals on my aging face.

Tunnels

(*In October, 2010, thirty-three Chilean miners were rescued
after being trapped in a mine collapse 2,300 feet below ground for more than sixty-nine days.*)

I watched, prayerfully, as they emerged
one by one
from that tight tunnel of salvation
newly bored half a mile into the earth
to pierce the roof of the dank, sultry space
that for months had threatened
to be the womb of death.

Thirty-three men in all—
throughout the long hours that brought night,
then day, then night again.
As each appeared—
some in cold light of desert night,
some in the blazing desert sun—
at the mouth of the tunnel
love, ever hopeful, waited for reunion.
Eyes moist with teary joy,
fingers pacing in anticipation,
hungry arms embraced the beloved
and fears dissolved.

Long before their desert deliverance,
these same thirty-three
had traveled through another tunnel
from dark and moist warm womb of life
into the radiance of day
where mother-love waited
in joy and hope
to caress and nurture
a cherished child.

Our lives are blessed with many tunnels,
those countless tunnels
that guide us from deep caves of sorrow
and draw us toward the light—
if we have will to follow—
to arise in new-found hope and purpose.

Do these but foreshadow the ultimate tunnel
to be opened by my final breath?
Will I fly through the dazzling spirit pathway,
emerge to find you, my love,
smiling, waiting to embrace me?
And, as you fold your arms about me,
will you whisper, "We are home."?

Under Rosemary

The comfort of the early summer garden
surrounds me, cocooned in pillow-soft lounge chair.
Lulled by tender sun, brow-kissing breeze and blue-draped sky,
I'm drawn into a waking reverie.
A sideways glance reveals,
tucked under spreading rosemary bush,
half covered by the fragrant branches,
a wooden shape.

Curiosity piqued, shifting from my chair,
I bend down and retrieve the weathered case.
Its vague familiarity resonates
with stirrings in my soul.

I caress the small treasure chest
sensing the wealth within.
My palms gently stroke the lid
as Aladdin with his lamp.

Suddenly, magically springing open,
it releases precious jewels
that rise, sparkling, into the air.
Floating opals and diamonds in rainbow hues,
prisms of light and delight
tease me with flashes of recognition,
fragments of fading lovely dreams.

Achingly, yearningly, I reach out
hoping to draw the shimmering gems to my heart.
Touched, they turn to watery tears
weeping across my startled fingers.

Searching skyward
I watch fleeting iridescent bubbles
escape toward the sun,
then disappear.
Closing the box,
I note the inscription
carved into the lid:
"Memories."

Vignette: The Forties, Brooklyn, NY

Wet pavement-dust smell twinges my nose.

Remember the city's summer showers?

Huddled in sweaty doorways,

peering through steamy glass

at rain-rays shaping Vs

in gutter puddles;

clammy, grey jump-rope clenched in one hand

bouncing the once-pink Spalding with the other

on the cool marble-tile floor.

"Look! It's letting up now."

Bursting out to sail our match-book boats,

running beside the sudden rivers

till the paper ships descend the corner sewer.

Waiting for Fireflies

Settling on my back porch in June's twilight,
I hope to see my harbingers of summer
display their brilliance across the backdrop of evergreens.
As the last vestige of blue sky melts into gray,
I wait for fireflies.

What feeds the soul has been grown
in the fields of memory,
and I recall the glorious displays
of years ago in night-black bushes
when I disowned the cruelty of youth
that stole their magic with a Mason jar.

Will they return this year to bring me cheer?
Ah! Finally a tiny blink of light and then another,
each flash a pinprick of joy,
but few and sparsely spread
across a wide expanse of trees,
and after a few minutes, all is dark.

It is the same with all the pleasures
of our younger days
that steadily diminish with advancing age.
But my fireflies tell me,
"Be happy with the smaller gifts;
they still are joys.
Greet them with a fleeting kiss,
but do not try to grasp them."

And as I count my years in summers past,
my future in summers yet to be,
I wonder how many Junes remain
for me to wait for fireflies.

Fran Karnish

This gathering of hearts, broken by death,
has become the place
where we add laughter to our tears.

Anna, at Sixteen

I look at you, my woman-child,
and all that I can see
is traces of your father.
Not a single trace of me.

My eyes peruse the raven locks,
the secrets in your dark brown eyes.
I know the quickness of your mind,
delighted that you're young, but wise.

Oh! But wouldn't I have loved to see
somewhere in you a part of me.

You catch me watching you and dart
A glance at me that strikes my heart.

You smile at me as though you know
that mothers sometimes have to show
their part in growing things of grace.
And then I look upon your face

The joy there can't be misconstrued.
Your loving is my part in you.

Dance Partner

Even with you gone, the music still moves me,
    causes my body to sway almost automatically
      to its contagious rhythm.

But my dance partner has left the room,
    left the dance floor, exited my life
      and relegated me to the listeners at the party.

I remember, too easily, the joyous abandon
    of being in your arms, held tightly,
      and gracefully led across the floor.

No one else existed, for those moments,
    no care dared to intrude
      into the space our bodies created.

How I enjoyed dancing with you,
    having you hold me and lead me
      across the room to swaying rhythms.

You took me dancing on our first date
    and I learned, very quickly,
      to follow where you led me, anywhere in life.

To follow you was natural.
    You loved me thoroughly and led me to places
      I never even knew I wanted to go.

But who will waltz with me now, who will hold me close?
    Who will lead my following heart to unexpected places?
      Will there ever be another partner, like you, for me?

I long for the security of the dance,
    for the steadiness and safety of your arms
      but settle in the space of the observer.

My heart must wait, as must my feet,
    to find new music to which to dance
      with unexpected partners that are still unknown.

Solitary Swim

I indulged myself today in an ocean swim.
It was the first, in many years, without you.
Whatever kept me away quickly melted
in the wake of its liquid serenity.

I surrendered easily to the tranquility.
The buoyancy of the water lifted me, held me,
and I recalled days in the past
of sparkling sunlight and sweet conversation.

Each year our entry into the warm summer ocean
was a milestone, a marker,
the beginning of a wondrous season
of sea and sun and escape from the realities of life.

There were favorite books reserved for the occasion,
music to uplift, soothe and savor,
intoxicating libations, sipped in water bottles, to escape detection
and, always, the wonderful promise of serenity.

Today I was alone.
The joys of summers past
were still vibrant in my memory and not to be forgotten,
but needed to be altered to suit my new circumstance.

I will now have to adjust. As difficult as it seems,
I must find new simple joys, single seaside delights.
I must allow the ocean to sustain me, to refresh me
and to replenish my desire to, once again, find pleasure in life.

Support Group

We come together,
  strangers, in pain so heavy
  we doubt another could comprehend.

But as we sit
  with controlled emotion to check our tears
  we hear the laments of other hearts.

Our own grief
  has broken our hearts
  and opened them to vulnerability

to acknowledge the pain
  of sisters and brothers
  whose loss is no less devastating.

We comfort each other,
  listen to the tales of progress and of woe
  and share the things that have helped us.

In an effort to help
  we tell our stories
  and remind each other of tomorrow.

And joyfully we laugh
  both at ourselves and each other
  telling of our own foibles in re-learning to live.

This gathering of hearts, broken by death,
  has become the place
  where we add laughter to our tears.

The Whistler

I heard someone whistling today,
   walking down the street,
   a joyful sound, almost a reverie.

And I remembered you,
   whistling through life,
   completely absorbed in whatever you were doing.

You sometimes whistled while we walked,
   through wooded areas, mostly,
   where reminiscence of your childhood inspired you.

You almost always whistled while you worked,
   like the dwarfs in Snow White,
   concentrated on the task before you.

Rollerblading also brought out the whistler in you.
   The freedom of soaring along paths in the park
   released not only your tension but jubilation as well.

You, who could not carry a tune,
   whistled splendidly
   each note you could not sing.

I recall myself smiling
   as you sang, off-key, in my ear,
   while you held me on the dance floor.

Whenever your heart could not contain
   the happiness within you,
   you broke out in melodic, joyous whistling.

Hardly anyone whistles anymore.
   It has become a lost art, but this day served its purpose.
   It reminded me of the simple joys still in my existence.

Inward Journey

Upon Remembering Wordsworth's
    "The World is Too Much With Us"

I need to be alone, sometimes,
to filter out the world,
to look within and
check my emotional temperature.

I need to be alone, sometimes,
when the music of life
has quieted and
joy has begun to elude me.

Then I must turn inward,
leave calendars and busyness behind
and seek out, once again,
the well-spring of calm within.

I must stir up my courage
to be firm against demands
which fill up only my time
and not the pleasures of my heart.

I need to be alone, sometimes,
to leave the herd and venture on my own
toward those quiet adventures
of the spirit and the soul.

I need to be alone, sometimes,
to check in, to write myself a mental note,
to email a validation to Fran on AOL ---
that all will be well.

So forgive me, world,
for sometimes saying "no"
to the whirlwind of life.
Sometimes, I need to be alone.

Barbara Pastorello

To write is to renew oneself
again and again,
and to give back
that which has been given

Again in My Dreams

You showed up again last night in that dream I always dream.

You were young, strong, tan and handsome as I remember you were in the early

days when life was easy.

You smiled that certain smile and looked at me in that certain way and I was so very

happy. I ran to you and you to me just like in the movies.

We spent a little time together, not enough; always not enough. I knew that

I was dreaming. I always do. I did not want to wake up.

I could have stayed asleep for the rest of my days,

but morning came as it always does and you vanished.

Those days when I awake from that dream are the hard days. I have to keep

from crying and pretend that all is well. In my heart is that familiar ache.

It's been five years since you died. You died on my birthday, a day I picked so your

suffering would end. The doctors thought me brave, but I was not. I told them to do

what they were telling me was necessary so you could leave in peace. It did not

matter if it was my birthday as all the days in that month would never be easy from then

on.

This year I will give a present to myself. I will pretend that you are near.

You know, I think you really are and that your spirit lives in me and gives me strength.

How else could I have survived this long?

Our Forever Painting

The painting on the wall of you and me

Brings back the most tender memory

Your arms around me and your head on my shoulder

There, in that painting, you shall never grow older

The love you show as you lean into me

Was a love so strong that it just had to be

I miss you, my darling, and I still need you here

But, you cannot answer and so flow my tears.

All Is Not Lost

All is not lost when you lose a love even though it will hurt so

All is not lost when you realize that you have miles that you must go

If all were lost, how could we go on and what would be our fate?

If we tried to make sense of anything what scale would we use to rate?

No, the essence of life is in the living even when all feels so wrong

And the life that's worth living must look for a song to move oneself along

Yes, the life that's worth living must think of the giving especially when one feels bereft

For in the giving, you find that the living is worth more than your heart could ever guess.

Crimson Flowers

Crimson flowers caress the ground and
Mother Nature makes no sound as
She bids the seasons 'round and 'round

The beauty of the world in fall
Cannot be matched, no not at all
The world seems ready for her sleep
As winter beckons with snow so deep

We each reflect on change as seasons come
And seasons go
As we, our memories arrange
We feel the highs and then the lows

So as we relive our days, and reminisce in many ways
The changing seasons need no praise
And life is good at our Fairways.

Giving Thanks

Thank you God for tea after afternoon naps
For friends who call and other caring chaps

For comfy chairs and quiet time
For books, and songs with all of their rhyme

For so much to do or nothing at all
For all kinds of weather

For the warmth of a shawl
For family and work or no work at all
For catching me whenever I fall

For singing birds and flowers in bloom
For giving me growing emotional room

For all the above and so very much more
I give you these thanks from deep in my core

Love Walks In

I heard your voice again my love

    it spoke hauntingly to me

        and once again I see

            your presence is trying to free

                me from all torments

                    which keep me dying here

                        with you.

Paradise Lost

In the beginning we seemed united
Like penguins on the icy tundra, we huddled together for warmth awaiting
Our turn at the inner circle praying for survival

Years passed slowly, yet were gone in an instant

Words never spoken cannot heal, but words uttered in anger can wound
the heart as an arrow finds its mark and digs deep

The travails continued endlessly

Two down, two to go

One word, addiction, took its toll on all.
It missed no one, like an octopuses' tentacles
it reached out to invade our lives

Crisis was normal
Sanity was not

Oh! The wasted hours and minutes when we might have sought love
Instead of harboring hate within our twisted souls.

Senior Thoughts

It's time to go shopping my buddy and me
We do it quite often, but not with much glee

The senior citizens of which we now number
Go down each aisle as if in a slumber

We can't see the prices because they're so small
We can't see the dates on the specials at all

We wander around as if shopping on Mars
We hope we don't upend the rows full of jars

We stand at the produce, where is all the help?
We can't find the onions, we can't find the kelp

We stand at the deli holding number eleven
Before it's our turn we might be in heaven

We look at the pet food, remember our furries
No longer with us except in our memories

And when we get home what do we find?
We left some food in the cart left behind

Now we are thinking why don't we 'phone
The Peapod number and just stay at home.

I Remember Papa

In the late 40's or 50's there was a show on TV called I Remember Mama. I loved it and watched it all the time.

I do not remember much about my Mama except that she was always working around the house - washing clothes on the washboard, or ironing in 90 degree weather with the sweat pouring off her face. She had to go on the roof to hang these clothes and I would try to help her. I also remember her going to Bingo often, sometimes twice in a day.

But, Papa I remember the most. Papa was what he called a Jack of all Trades man. I never really knew what he did for a living. When the teacher would inquire of me his profession (they did that back in the day) I would just look at her blankly and not have an answer. Because at different times Papa was a rigger in the Brooklyn Navy Yard, a painter, (I remember looking up at our building one day and seeing him on a scaffold painting away. It was terrifying to watch,) he was a cement mason, a brick layer, a cab driver and a superintendent of an apartment house in Bay Ridge where I was born. He also sold rags at night because he was embarrassed to do this in the day. He was always trying to scrape money together to make our lives a little better. He had 4 mouths to feed plus my mother and him.

I remember him talking to a tenant in our building and smelling Vicks in the hall. This woman had 5 or more children and so I guess one of them was always sick with a cold. In those days Vicks was the go to product for congestion as not many could afford to see a doctor. I remember my own mother wrapping my chest in a warm, flannel scarf or blanket after putting on Vicks Vapor Rub underneath and then tucking it all under my pajamas. I could sleep better then when I was sick. To this day whenever I see a Vicks Vapor Rub bottle or smell that scent I think of that woman.

My dad was an alcoholic, but he was also a caring man. He did his best always to provide for us under the most difficult circumstances. I guess the term for him was functioning alcoholic. He taught himself to do algebra and to read blueprints in hopes of improving his lot in life.

I often wonder what he could have accomplished were he not an alcoholic. But, I did love him and I do remember Papa.

Giving In And / Or Up

There are days that I cannot remember where I left anything and I believe
    it's getting worse

It seems as though I've lost my mind and memory and it feels much
    like a curse

Where did I put this or that, it takes so much energy and time to
    simply figure out where I lost my mind

Or what it was I lost this time.

Will it get better overall - I really have to doubt
    I have no recourse and apparently, no clout

I need to study memory tricks to find whatever it is
    I've missed

But doesn't one need a memory to learn the memory
    tricks?

Forgive me whilst I complain it is so annoying as you can see
    I'll let you know how it turns out, but it won't be easy-peasy

When I find what I'm looking for what joy and rapture it will be
    But until then I need to sit and stare at things, you see.

If I'm lucky with this memory game, I'll find all that I'm missing
    But, right now, to myself I am not even listening!

Wrinkles

My wrinkles are deep, but some are light
I have put up with them without a fight
But then those commercials drew me in
To now look your age is considered a sin

I will not try Botox, uh, uh, not me
It was bad enough that I got new knees
The ads always promise me all kinds of stuff
But I know when to say enough, enough!

To pay the price they want and demand
For one tiny jar that is lost in my hand
To erase those many wrinkles I will moan
I would seemingly have to float a loan

No, thanks I will keep them you see
That's fine with me, and besides they're free.

Melancholia

The sun has left the sky, no golden hues remain
For now, the clouds appear and after, comes the rain

My heart feels not the sun nor clouds of rain it seems
Because I know how fate has stolen all my dreams

This day will come and go as all the others have
And for my hurting soul there seems to be no salve

I only ask for strength for mine, I think, has left
My love has gone away and so I am bereft

All our memories I've safely kept
And with that brings a smile

And I know my love would want me to
Go that extra mile.

Brain Fog

I was talking to myself, as I often do, and came to the conclusion that my brain needs help.

I see my brain as a large room full of little people wandering around and most are looking for a door of escape. Those remaining little people are holding "Help Wanted" signs and are also looking around for some relief.

I can actually feel my brain cells dying. It is not painful, thank God, but rather bizarre and rather frightening yet comical at the same time.

I have begun to forget so many things, including where I put stuff, that I have chosen not to fight or rally against the inevitable, but to simple accept that I am not young anymore and cannot do what I used to do even though I put up a good front.

So if you see me looking confused, please just pass me by and remember that I am, indeed, confused. Do not offer help of any kind although I am appreciative of that. Instead, just shake your head in sympathy and look me straight in the eye and nod that you understand. That is the only bromide that I require.

Thank you for your kindness.

A Dog's Life

The little girl looked out the door and saw the dog a running
Why did he do this she would think, what did he see a coming?
She watched this on and off, and again and again he ran
Once toward town and back again; she already named him Sam

A dog's life is a dog's life she thought most every time
Much like Daddy said, "This life is just a grind."
One day when I'm all grown up I'll run away like Sam
Except I am in braces and my legs don't work a damn

But once I have my freedom, I'll finally see this world
If only off to town and back to see the flags unfurled
For I can also live a dog's life and it may not be so bad
I cannot move a lick or two and so sometimes I'm sad

So say a prayer for me if you would be so kind
I'm gonna walk someday, you'll see. I just made up my mind.

Leather Recliner

She lowered herself into the brown, leather recliner which stood in the corner of the family room. The chair which she bought for him. She leaned back and elevated her legs which were hurting now from the cold day. She glanced to her right and saw through the sunroom into the double doors to the patio and garden.

The wind was starting to whip up the leaves which had fallen from her favorite trees in the backyard, and it appeared for a moment as if it was raining leaves. They were glorious in their colors, competing; it seemed, with one another for attention. The reds were not just red, but scarlet, the honey-gold and the yellow and tangerine danced in the whirlwind created by the strong breezes. She loved watching them.

When, she wondered, did the leaves die? Was it when they left the mother tree or when they fell to the earth? These were her thoughts then. Time to contemplate, time to relax and let the mind wander off in any direction, perhaps to some faraway place found only in her mind.

He never had any real time to use that chair. Time to think, time to plan the rest of her life - without him. And the leaves started it all.

Unknown

The words creep into my mind like shadows on the wall
But, I do not write them down

For who would care if I record these thoughts that swing
Back and forth as the flag swings on a windy day and sometimes
Rolls over and over the pole on which it hangs getting twisted
In the wind -- round and round

I feel as if I can fly away, but only in my mind for I am
Tethered to some unknown thread waiting for it to break

Crash

One word - crash has many meanings.
I took this word and did this with it.

CRASH - Cars smashing into each other.
Sounds of agony, suffering and pain.
Accidents are never planned.
Should have been on high alert.
Never trust the other driver to do the right thing.
Too late now.
Ambulance sounds in the distant.
Hospital halls and stretchers and who knows what else.

CRASH - Stocks plummeting.
Fears of recession, depression all over again.
Once was not enough?
Bread lines?
Apples on a corner?
Bad memories not likely to leave soon.
It will take years to fix this mess.
Blood pressure rising.

CRASH - Tired, depleted energy.
Looking for a rest - a nap - a room of quiet.
No lights, no sound, just blissful sleep if it will come.
You can crash anywhere these days.

CRASH - Damn computers!
Sometimes more trouble than they are worth.
So dependent now.
Cannot do business the old way anymore.
It was slower for sure, but reliable.
People not connecting on a personal level anymore either.
Sad. Soon, I fear, people will stop speaking in words and start to use numbers.
Is there an app for that?

With apologies to Clement Clarke Moore

I looked out my window and what should I see?

But a fiery red cardinal perched on my tree

His beak was quite shiny, his coat silky smooth

And, thus, seeing this changed my once sour mood

And I smiled as I saw him alight from my tree

I wished him good flying and then watched him flee

As he flew quickly away as if on a mission

I wished him God's speed and then had to dismiss him

Her Feline

He barely moved, but his eyes looked like devil eyes with an orange glow
He leaped upon the table as she placed her keys there and turned on the lights

He nudged against her, purring that beautiful sound
She knew he was happy that she was finally home

And so was she

Now she would bask in unconditional love after a long, hard day
and she was once again forever grateful for that one feline

Techno Phobia

In this day and age I do not belong
I have no Ipod to hear the songs

I don't compute, I can't Ipad
I'm lost and lonely and very sad

I don't know from Wii, it does not exist
I can't text messages, so please don't insist

I can barely navigate my own smart 'phone
Tell me please, that I'm not alone

My microwave buzzes, my dishwasher sings
My car even talks to me among other things

My computer really hates me, it does not obey
What does it want from me anyway?

All the techies will try to add to my list
And I keep trying to resist and resist

Please bring back the peace, the quiet of days
The days gone by where my serenity stays

If there any more gadgets for me to reject
I'll stay in dinosaur land, and just be a wreck.

A Sailor and a Love

'Twas a tale was told to all the sailors who live their lives on the sea
'bout a lonely girl who walked on the beach singing of times to be

She fell deeply in love with handsome man, the man who came ashore
And they pledged their eternal love to each forever and evermore

The sailor and the maiden both believed they would be man and wife
And though he had to sail once more he dreamed of their beautiful life

But the waves claimed his ship as the wind did blow and took her down in the angry sea
None were saved and none were mourned more than her handsome he

And so she waits and waits on the beach while singing a mournful tune they say
And night after night you can hear her sing as she prays and prays and prays

Come back to me my sailor man and let us begin our new life
Please come home again and see that I'm ready to be your wife

No one can tell here he will not return for she would never think this true
And so she walks on the beach and waits for there is nothing she can do

So if you love a sailor man be aware of the pits and falls
'Lest you spend your life just waiting and hoping and wishing for his call

For Children Only

Hi Kids:

This is a letter to you both from your sometimes cheery, sometimes gloomy mother on the pitfalls of growing old. Notice I did not say older, but old. Here's hoping you get there; it is so much fun.

1. You will not like looking old. You will walk crooked some of the time or else list to one side or the other. You will be mistaken for a drunk. Do not be concerned as you will have plenty of company.

2. You will often drop things; they will simply slip from your fingers. You will then have to bend to pick up these things and that can become tricky due to your lack of balance. So be prepared to fall gracefully. Practice that until you get it right.

Your handwriting will become shaky, but do not be concerned. Again, plenty of company.

3. You will forget a host of things. O.K., most things. Your Hippocampus (the part of the brain that stores memory) will shrink to the size of a pea and that will be your excuse. Also, whatever skills you possess will need shoring up regularly lest they also leave you. And 'phone numbers and passwords will have to be kept near, especially in times of stress.

4. Faces and names will become a blur. Don't even try. Just smile and look bewildered which will be your state of mind most of the time anyway.

5. Your sense of smell and hearing are up for grabs. So far, I am doing well with these and I hope you will too.

6. You may still travel if you are lucky. Otherwise, invest in videos as that will be your only way to see the world. That, and the internet.

7. Your children will ask dumb questions of you. Be patient as I have been when you are asked on your answering machine "Where are you?" "You should be home by now", etc. "How are you feeling?" Do not answer that last question honestly or they will send ambulances.

9. Get permission from your children if you need to deviate from your normal schedule. They worry so, God bless them.

Hope this does not sound too depressing. It is just a resignation (took me three minutes to recall that word) as to getting old. It can be fun if you pal around with friends who have the ability to laugh at themselves. I know I do.
Happy aging!

Joan Saunders

To Poetry – With Love

You are my solace
my tranquility
the respite from daily angst

my safe harbor
my constant sanctuary
the private addiction of my mind

Invisible Truth

I write this not as an epitaph to life,
but as a genuine fair warning to all nubile females
in their thirties and forties, wearing Manolo's
bought on E-Bay, clutching fake Fendi's,
comfortable in their invincible skins,
because they don't know, yet
that they will become invisible.

I read once, words of a wise woman
who recommended the CIA, MI5 and other covert
organizations, hire only women in their sixties.
They'd be far more successful on stealth missions
as they cannot be seen by the majority of the western world -
particularly the male gender.

A strange osmosis begins as you approach the sixth decade.
You won't notice at first, until the teller looks past
you to the next thirty something in line - the bagger
at the checkout packs groceries for a forty something
ahead of you - turns and walks away, following
his Gucci loafers and firm muscles in tight jeans.

In a few more years the fade to blank begins.
Breasts, hips, lips, all melt away and disappear.
Soon, only sixty plus females will greet your sighting.
They know you're holding this heavy burden
that you cannot yet lay down.

The male has a stay for about a decade
on this invisibility - but forty something
in his tight jeans and Gucci loafers will come to realize
his own burden, heavy in his arms – virility, pride, ego
weigh much and he must lay them down -

watching as they dissipate to fine dust, precarious
with each slight disturbance of air – while thirty something,
with her peach perky breasts and honeydew buttocks,
unaware of his presence, carelessly sneezes
as she passes.

Things I Don't Do Anymore

I don't get out of bed easy.
I used to wake early, before the alarm –
now my hand darts out, like a sleeping serpent
disturbed, slapping the buzzer
four or five times.

I don't do dishes after dinner.
They pile in the sink, sometimes for days –
dried on crud glaring admonishment,
which I ignore until someone is visiting.
I don't take out the trash at night or go through
the mail daily – it lies on the counter,
filed in the 'in transit' section for a week
along with other 'I'll get to it' items –

a single white sock left after the dryer ate
its partner, black sweat pants, tie resting on top,
waiting to be guided through the waistband,
an assortment of advertisement flyers
that I thought I would call on –
whiter teeth in just one visit, two
dollars off my next grocery delivery
(though I don't get them delivered),
dirt cheap car insurance (in New Jersey?) –

a green fleece I borrowed, waiting for weeks
to be returned and all those lists I make
with good intention, hiding between the final
sale 75% off catalogues. I don't do windows,
I don't do floors, I don't clean out closets
until I can't close the doors – I don't clean off
the guest room bed until they're actually arriving –

I don't get pedantic about dust balls under the table
or frantic when twelve are coming to dinner –
life's irritating small stuff I don't sweat at all
and never do I cry over spilt milk –
isn't that what paper towels are for?

Making Tapenade

I drive ten miles
on a balmy Saturday,
while it's still freshly quiet,
before weekday workers
make their jaunty ritual to the mall,

to the best Italian market - the one
where Hugo, with hair black
and slick as a magpies back, oozes
promises with the delicacies
he serves. He knows, without a word,
what I need; not Italian – it's

the Greek, pitted Kalamata
olives. Their embodiment escapes
to the slippery roundness –
not all black, the deepest red
and mauve tinge the plumpness.

Taking the biggest garlic cloves,
I squash hard with a wide blade knife
to release the aroma.
Curly parsley and capers
of a fleshy frog green. The oil,

still a virgin, embraces all, escaping
onto fingers, face, on that stray strand of hair.
The pungent mixture surrounds,
arouses the senses, enflames
the appetites.

Oh, the rich tangy smoothness
tantalizes on strong aged Asiago
cheese, on beef or ham.
It will awaken a cold fish
or lay blanketed with lasagna
and is an emollient spread for dark bread.

But, take care -
this concoction is known
to cause the blurred vision of gluttony,
lone midnight excursions into addiction,
blatant diet abuse and a certain type of mania.

One Picture of Mother.

I have only one picture of you.
The sepia and cream of you.
Buttoned up coat with fake fur collar,
a small hat – dark hair fresh with permanent
for your holiday. The only holiday
you'd had in more than twenty years. This picture,
with Aunt Mabel. Two widows
holding the pose for the seaside
photographer on the promenade at Blackpool.
Eight weeks later, you were gone –
gone from me at thirteen,
with a lifetime ahead
and left wondering.

I'm still wondering.
What would you think
of me now – this middle aged woman.
Wondering, if had you lived
and raised me past thirteen,
would I still be living in that small
village in the mid-west of England?
Would I have married some local boy,
now, at this age, with his Potteries twang
and beer belly hanging like extra pie crust
over his belt – with a gaggle of kids
and grandkids around me. Would I have stayed
with him?

Wondering, would I be like you -
downtrodden, thick stockings, sensible shoes -
happy for a game of dominoes,
a bottle of beer and bag of crisps at the pub
on a Saturday night?
Would I have escaped?
Would I have wanted more?
Or, would I have been happy to bask
in your nurture – keeping me close, holding
my life a willing prisoner to yours,
with the same small hopes
and unmet expectations?

The Blessing of the Leaves

Maybe it was the feeling
of early fall – bright and blustery
with that first frosty nip
glancing across tips
of recently cut grass, leaving
a sparkling glaze
that had yet to succumb to the day's
warming. Crows swooped,
circling – their wild clarion caw
signaling the season, and the roar
of a high wind ripping across the tops
of Lilly Mountain, its voice bellowing
to the gods of nature.
My small house nestles
on the hip of the rocks
below – and I, in hot water
in the tub on my deck –
drifting in sublime comfort of heat,
peace and mindlessness –
and the morning sun broke
through swaying boughs dressed
in autumn. The wind left
its high peak, came plummeting
down in a blast of fury to bereft
the trees – flailing
to let loose a storm of gold.
I rose from the water,
dripping in my nakedness,
arms raised to receive
the sacrament of the sun,
the blessing of the leaves
swirling in their delirium,
clothing me in a coat
of many colors.

Fall Back – A Sestina.

It is one hour
after waking. The clock says nine
but is it really eight?
Did I forget to fall back
in the night? Am I an hour ahead
of myself?

I feel quite beside myself,
as it were - an extra hour
to live over, to get ahead.
Could I be like the cat with nine
lives, that longs to go back,
but never wants to get past eight?

Think now – whatever I just ate
for breakfast, while I was not myself,
before I go back
to get the extra hour,
I could eat over again. Nine
mini-muffins comin' up, 'cause I'm still ahead!

Wait a minute! If I did that because I'm ahead,
it could add eight
inches to my hips, or even nine.
This being beside myself
is not so great! The extra hour
is confusing. I'm not going back!

So, if I don't go back
before I thought I was ahead,
before I had that extra hour,
it wouldn't be eight
and I wouldn't feel beside myself,
it would still be nine,

and if it's nine
and I haven't gone back
to indulge myself
in the extra muffins, I'm still ahead –
I haven't added eight
inches to my hips…and I don't have an extra hour!

But, alas, it is not nine and I am ahead!
One look at my cell phone tells me I have to go back. It is eight
and I am myself. Where's the duct tape? I need it for this extra hour.

Attack of the Cyber Demons

There once was a woman
who suffered gravely
at the teeth and claws
of the cyber demons.
Those invisible predators infiltrated
through her windows
gobbled up all her cookies
and even emptied her cache.

They preyed upon her each day
and into the night until she could no longer
browse though her grayed out
windows and needed to refresh
herself constantly,
so she sent a message in an instant
to the cyber doc.

He diagnosed a virus,
a despicable worm
had wiggled its way in, invaded
her mailbox, which was sitting
outside her walls of fire, on its bright red
post, minding its own business
and cuddled up to its buddy
Spam

Then the book of face-
making, that guided her very
existence went into deep freeze
and wouldn't budge from its home-
page – and the demons
constantly popped up,
blocking all her options,
with error, error, error –
until she was so distraught
she just had to escape.

She searched through those icons
of power, until she pointed
and cursored at what she saw
over the top of her desk. Her husband's
picture, plastered on her wallpaper,
lost its color and flashed – system
failure, system failure! At this
she dragged and dropped herself
to the bed…and crashed!

Symphony of the Snow

Here it comes again,
drifting in like a melody
you thought you'd dug out
of your mind. White crystal notes,
starting slowly, floating like music
from the sky – one small C sharp,
a larger B flat,
then the entire scale of E major
hits your windows
and before you know it
the full blown orchestra comes
booming down, pelting you
with Tchaikovsky's 1812 Overture.

You switch on to hear
another eight inches predicted -
the GS Parkway is closed again,
don't park on local streets
or your car could be lost
beneath Rachmaninoff's 3rd Piano Concerto –
and you know how long that lasts.
Just relax, stay home – take
a snow day – step out-
side to start shoveling
and let Beethovan's 5th Symphony
kiss your face.

Coming Home to Shropshire in the Spring

What I notice first
after being away so long, is the green.
There is no green anywhere like this green –
soaked with spring rain, blessed with warm sun,
the deep color leaps off the landscape, shocking
my eyes with its intensity. As I pass meadows,
I envy the life of cows, grazing in contentment –

and I am absorbed by the ordinary ecstasies –
the roll of fields dipping down into valleys,
old farmhouses in the distance, roadside cottages,
neat with flowering window boxes,
the smell of hay, long stored in barns.
Rough stone walls alongside
narrow country lanes.

Waking to the smell of bacon,
to smoky kippers, to hot black tea and toasted
Hovis bread slathered in farm butter
and the familiar Shropshire twang in voices
beneath my window. Old men on corners,
pipes dangling, talking through aromatic clouds
of burning tobacco.

The livestock market with the indecipherable call
of the auctioneer, and red-faced farmers,
port wine bellies hanging over britches,
green Wellington boots to the knee.
That tangible sense of permanence
under every cobble stone, in each ancient arch –
and as I catch my own green image in a shop window,
I watch centuries passing through me.

Easter Sunday

Always, we hoped for no rain –
a nice day for the parade.
Boys, like shrunken fathers in miniature
Sunday suits, tussled hair parted, slicked
with Brilliantine, starched collars,
black shined shoes, a carnation
in the button hole holding precariously.
Mothers cajoled, beguiled, nudging gently,
keeping the line-up straight.

Girls, hovered – small versions of their mother's
past youth with Shirley Temple curls, ringlets,
or braids shining, swept to crown,
held fast with a satin bow. Posies
dangling from inexperienced hands.

The dresses were the thing –
the hoped for envied bliss each girl waited
an entire year to wear. The one time,
most often, we could wear new.
No hand-me-downs this day.
No cast-offs. No sixpenny shoes
from the second hand shop.

This was the day my Mother excelled.
A year of scrimping resulted for me,
in the ultimate dress - the dress
this young girls heart had waited for.
Swathed in celery green taffeta,
a stiff net petticoat, stand up collar,
puff sleeves, large patch pockets
with delicate trellis work,
I slipped my finger tips through.

It was my first Sunday
in the grown up's church choir.
I stood, resplendent, joyous,
my young voice soaring high and clear.
'Morning has broken, like the first morning.
Blackbird has spoken, like the first bird.'
I was the bird – flying high, exalted,
floating away on a cloud of celery green
to a different place.

All We Can Do is Listen

Everything
has its time.
The moth, with paper wings,
beats its life away against a lighted
window pane.
Water turns to vapor.
An embryo begins.
From birth, we fly
through time heedlessly.
Choices encircle -
drawing on our essence,
exposing pain –
turning years to rising
smoke.
I weep for those
with ungrateful souls -
for when mind has gone
and every tip of every nerve
is dulled and our fog filled
brain seeks consolation –
thankfulness is all that remains.
And when time opens
its amazed mouth,
all we can do
is listen.

Inappropriate Behavior

Through this haze
of memory, I don't recall much
about my father –
his band of wispy grey hair, the aroma
of St Bruno Flake tobacco,
his gold watch and chain, slung low
across the belly of his waistcoat.
I can't see his face in my mind, remember
his features – the slant of his jaw,
the rise of his brow. I don't recall
his smile or how I felt
when he touched me.
My father left
before I really knew him –
when I say left, I mean
he died – he eighty, I eight.
I do recall
the day we buried him.
I wore a brand new brown and gold
tweed coat with velvet collar
and matching beret
and I was wildly waving
to Sylvia Taylor
my best friend
as our funeral car passed - excited,
it was my first time
in a car and I was wearing new clothes.
Mother reached out,
firmly lowered my hand
and gave me a disapproving look
I'd never seen before.

The Man At The Traffic Light In The Bright Red Sports Car

It was summer
as I drove my car through town.
My mind was elsewhere
when I pulled up to a traffic light. Idling,
waiting for the change
and consumed with what not,
and what to. Leaning on the open window,
not noticing how the sun caught the side
mirror and sparked off in a hundred
different directions. Not noticing
school children laughing, clowning
around on the sidewalk. Not noticing the glow
touching leaves, touching brilliant color
of flower pots outside stores, touching
faces, touching all those faces. Not noticing
the bright red sports car pulled up to my left
and the handsome man looking my way.
"You should smile more," he said.
His words shocked me out
of my trance, and I caught his eyes—Deep
brown, glinting with humor.
"You're beautiful—smile."
The light changed,
traffic moved, and he was gone.
How could he know about the divorce
attorneys, the debt collectors looking to take
what I didn't have?
All he wanted was a smile.

Tongue Lashing.

He looked like an ordinary man.
I alone knew his weapon.
It lay, unnoticed by others
inside the smooth, silken fissure
of his mouth
hidden by a handsome face – guarded
behind a row of whiter than white
teeth.

In company, it would sneak out
and slowly wrap its long slippery
length around my neck -
Taking my breath,
gaging me from revealing
too much.

At any time of day or night
it would whip out and slap
me hard, insisting I repair
my make-up, add the blood red
lipstick to my lips, brush
and rearrange my hair

or it would tether me by the ankle
to thrash mercilessly, if my shoes
weren't at least four inch stilettos.
It even added two letters
to my name and deducted five
years from my age.

It lay, preying
inside the bitter cage
of his mouth, waiting
to lash me into shape –
a shape of his very own
design.

The Blessed Boy

His Mother brought him
to the office to meet
the girls – young women
in the twenties and thirties.

He stood there -
his smile reaching
from ear to ear,
charismatic blue eyes

fringed with dark silken
lashes and a summer tan.
Oh, he was handsome -
and he knew it.

His face tilted slightly
upwards to receive
the glow. The sky broke
open and the blessed light
of adoration lay on his face

like a sun beam - bathing
him with the radiance
of knowing,
of finding his omnipotence.

Though only thirteen,
this was the power
he knew he would have
for a lifetime.

The Basket

When I was thirteen, it was the thing for young girls to carry their belongings – books, money purse, fountain pen, pencils and other personal items, back and forth to school, in a basket – just a regular market basket. There never seems to be any rhyme or reason to what becomes the 'in' thing – the latest fashion craze or 'hip' possession. This fad lasted a couple of years and thinking back on it now, it wasn't at all practical. My sixteen by twelve basket, deep by eight inches, with a wide arched handle across the width, was awkward and open for all to see my guarded girlish possessions. I remember it cost five shillings, which was a lot of money for me then. The basket is sturdy and made from tightly woven willow, two-tone brown and smooth as an aged stone and it never did splinter to thrust broken tips through my young skin.

It has stayed with me through decades – the only thing that has. The sudden holder of nightgown, slippers and bed jacket the night my son decided to arrive in this world in a hurry. It has served as the 'in-tray' on my desk for papers, held logs at an open fireplace, held books at the foot of my bed. It has endured with me, through marriages, childbirths and a one way trip across the Atlantic. Here it lays now, this five-shilling basket –on its side in my decorative display of stylish bric-a-brac on a high shelf, in the company of a brass candle stick with a long green candle, a cracked pot that once held Stilton, four old books from an antique store with titles I no longer remember, and some kind of Greek urn, from who knows where. Here it lays - its old, comfortable brownness, just the same. Finally at peace, beside a vintage bottle of Chardonnay.

Amber-Eyed Demons of the Night

In Van Gogh's great picture, The Starry Night,
the skies breath swirls and whirls
in deepest blues and gold – scrolling up over
the blue mountains, beyond the blue village,
below the asylum window
where he lay, his tortured mind pushing the rush
of night around the moon, circling stars,
closely missing the church steeple, roofs of houses,
branches of the Cypress swaying away
from the colossus of his amber-eyed demons
rolling in, out of the night sky –
in Van Gogh's great picture, The Starry Night.

Love

Love starts
weightless –
light as a glance
and then gone.
Only to return heavier
when eyes meet eyes again.
It hangs unsure,
on the first word -
stumbling ungainly
into conversation –
into the brush of hand
against hand
into question and answer
into when
into now
gaining weight
with lips upon lips
flesh touching flesh
until it becomes the whole
weight
of your
world

Sanderlings

The undercurrent
roar and lighter swooshing
of the ocean is constant.

This continuous sound
does not disturb - rather,
it lulls and soothes, as I walk

barefoot on the beach, day after day -
early, at the very edge
where water meets sand.

Waves break -
rushing in, pushing
the last white froth over my feet,

while I watch these comical little birds,
their breasts bursting pure white,
wings the color of wet stones.

Like wind up mechanical toys
on black short sticks -
back and forth - go and stop short,

following each retreating wave.
Probing wet sand to snatch
small crabs and worms

exposed by the washing,
then retreating swiftly,
before the incoming rush.

Their tiny legs moving faster
than an eye can see -
white froth chasing their tails.

Resurrection of the Pothos

I cannot kill
this Pothos plant –
forgetting to water, leaving it high and dry
on its shelf. I can hear it whimpering
when I pass, as it droops and gasps its last breaths.
I take pity and throw in a glass full.
Thirty minutes later, it has risen
like Lazarus.
It calls to me from its deep green throat -
not this time lady! Not this time!

The Pleading

(On the last morning after the Frost Place Poetry Festival)

After flat black, night breaks –
limbs stretch in a bed not mine for the last time.
The refrigerator coils in the corner
slow breathing – a two-note pulsing
of the fan overhead – muffled
sounds from behind the wall -
an obsessive sense of awareness
invades, incarcerates.

Frost, Dickinson, Hardy – all of them
and all of now, rampage through my brain.
Words, order of words, the benign meaning
or malignant consequence – cause and effect.
Lines form and break, colliding
with here and now and tomorrow –
waiting for her – my fickle muse
to bring her soothing little cup to my mouth

Life is a Man with a Handsome Face -

- and he hangs out at this bar called Good Intention.
Early in my years, as I was passing by this corner joint,
the monkey on my back, named Curiosity, nipped my ear
and said – *Go on...go on...ya know you want to* –
so I poked my head inside, and before my adolescent eyes
could adjust to the glorious glow of his presence, he spoke –
*You shouldn't be in here girl – you're too young,
but since you are, come on in – drag up a stool,
let me tell you a thing or two.*

I wasn't ready to meet Life yet,
but there he was – his handsome face beguiling,
a devious glint sparked in his eyes. Curiosity nipped again.
I sidled in and sat down, close.
His charismatic smile would melt stone to molten ore -
and I was in awe. He pulled out a book, all shiny and new,
and slapped it down. It had my name on the cover.
Opening it, he took a pen from his pocket
and with a sly smile he said – *Well now, let's see
what I can come up with for you, little girl –
I'm going to write how it will be.
You will have to take whatever I choose
to dish out.*

*I can make it hard or I can make it easy,
but easy is the road to go. All you have to do
is comply - give in - lay down - let me roll right over you.*
My eyes narrowed, my belly tightened, as young as I was,
no one was going to roll over me!
Anger and an enormous strength bubbled up
and my caldron of self will erupted.
With one swift, sure movement, my hand thrust out
and I grabbed Life by the throat – yanked him
off that bar stool and dragged him, screeching and yelping,
through the door – running, hell bent towards what
I didn't know.

Racing wild, I passed building after building -
on each door a sign hung, with the same word 'decades.'
I paid no mind – just kept hauling that Life,
kicking and screaming behind. *You'll never make it.
You'll trip, you'll fall,* he said.
And I did, many times – bruising Pride, crushing Ego,
but side stepping Uncertainty.

There were times when I fell hard
and knocked my heart right out of me
and it broke into pieces.
Anguish would kick it to the side and leave it,
whimpering. Sometimes, years would pass
before I could pick it up, pat it gently back
into shape and return it to its rightful place.

Then just as I thought I'd got Life whipped
and he didn't feel quite so heavy, didn't struggle
as much anymore – the road ahead lay thick
with a dense grey mist and suddenly veered off
in a different direction. A huge, black pit,
known as Depths of Despair, opened before me and I fell in –
free falling down and down into that dark place,
until I hit bottom. Life lay there beside me, weak,
helpless. His handsome face pallid, his glow
almost extinguished.

It was then I heard a soft whisper in the dark,
which became louder and louder, until it reverberated
in my ears. It was Resilience still sitting there
on my left shoulder and Resourcefulness on my right.
Come on, you can do it! They said. *You always have.
Pick yourself up and drag that Life with you
and get the hell out of here.*

That was a while ago now and I have moved on
up this road a long way. Curiosity still keeps nipping,
I'm happy to say, and Resilience and Resourcefulness
never leave my side. As for Life – well, I don't have
to drag him anymore - he comes easy, he's malleable –
we've become good friends -
so instead of the firm grip I had on him,
I placed a soft, velvet collar on his willing neck,
with a long, silken leash that I can loose out
or pull in, at will.

Newsflash! Osama bin-Laden Dead - May 1st, 2011

On any summer day
in Manhattan
the steaming streets run rich
with glistening diamonds –
gathered, wet and dripping
from the brow of sidewalk
hawkers – running down
air conditioned cold
café windows – hanging,
in real-time, on fingers
of uptown girls – the only
relief from their acknowledged
uniform of the city – black,
the color worn by the authentic
Manhattanite –

and the hot smell
of money mingles
with sewer gases, hotdogs,
pretzels – the occasional whiff
from a sleeping body
beneath cardboard
piled in a doorway –
the aromatic distinction
of marijuana from huddles
in alleyways, and the mélange –
the honk, buzz, screech, slam, thwak,
white noise against the black –

and on that brilliant
late summer morning, we watched
small, black silhouettes drop
from tall buildings – that spewed flashing
red with billowing clouds
of grey, that came before
black veils –
yet the city lives,
has an under-life
that sustains and rises
like Lazarus – never dead,
just dormant.
A decade later – no one
wears black
for the perpetrator.

Waiting for the Gift

The misted moon
hangs low,
haloed, heavy, barely able
to hold the weight.
Thoughts are ripped
from the bedrock
of the snow predicted
to start before midnight.
In the brain, pulsing
forward
a strange eerie silence.
The train whistle
frozen mid-blow –
seeping quickly.
The breath choked
through eye
sockets
of the diesel engines
on the highway.
All creatures,
slipping down
human and inhuman
waiting feebly
for the sky
to wet the tongue-
living, waiting
to release – pulling
the rip cord –
discarding
the manna on us
as if a gift.

To Poetry – With Love

You are my solace
my tranquility
the respite from daily angst

my safe harbor
my constant sanctuary
the private addiction of my mind

my emotional watershed
my life's release
the serene essence of my soul

my self-soothing
my faithful companion
the nurture for the inner child

my secret passion
my drug of choice
the heady elixir of my senses

You… are the poetry in my heart

Marion Stavitsky

There is a moment when my new poem
comes alive, and I read it carefully over and over,
to give it a name,
until I decide to simply call it "A Gift".

After My Granddaughter's Visit

Whose socks these are I think I know,
Her visit ended days ago,
But every time she waves "good-bye"
I'm sure something escaped her eye.

For years I've mailed the item found
Beneath the bed or on the ground.
"Please check once more" became my mantra,
"Look in the drawers and closets, can't ya"?

She calls to ask if she left her rings
But I can't keep mailing forgotten things!
"You know we love you very much
And always want you to be in touch

And visit us both day and night –
But the postal rate is out of sight!
Perhaps a list of items brought
Can be carefully checked so I'm not overwrought?"

I call to tell her "I'll mail your socks
But this is it – we've used our last box!"
She promises to take more care
And save me extra work (that's fair).

"Okay", she says," I'll be much better
"But, Nona, when you read can you see each letter?
 'Cause you left your glasses at our house
And I think the dog just found your blouse.

So please be patient and try not to mock –
I'm just a little "chip" off my grandma's block!"

Alaska

What god or goddess thought you up
And hurled the ice that formed the majestic glaciers

That appear like glistening giants robed in blue spires of ice?
They defy description until we mortals catch our breath

And, mouths open at the sight, hear the white thunder
From which you have cleverly created icebergs and fiords

And we gasp at what you have wrought
You have offered gold, copper, giant trees for lumber,

Salmon, trout, berries, brown bears, caribou herds, sheep,
Wolves, grazing moose, haughty eagles perched atop giant trees

Who look down on us with superior disdain – we who cannot fly
Your people are hardy and self-reliant, perhaps learning from

The native Tlingit Indians so skilled in crafts and giant totems –
perhaps built in homage to the powers who gave them Alaska.

Many years ago, Russia grabbed your wealth and beauty but
Was not astute enough to embrace you forever, and so you are
Part of us. And your wild beauty will remain unrivaled forever.

The Magic Of Albert Hall

If you want to hear the twang of a Bluegrass Song,
And you love to stomp your feet when you sing along,

When the banjo joins in and your chair begins to rumble
Better hold on tight so you don't begin to tumble!

Soon the sweetness of the dulcimer carries you away,
And the fiddle sneaks in and you want so much to play,

If you haven't been there yet, you should not delay,
It's the place to go--there is nothing more to say!

The Workers

Early in the morning
From my sunroom windows
I watch the brown-skinned men
Mow my lawn and sweep away
Nature's debris of dead, wrinkled leaves.

Intent on their tasks,
Heads covered with brimmed caps or "hoodies",
To shield them from the blazing sun.
They seem unaware of anyone as they move
Endlessly, staring at the grass from house to house.

The birds have silenced their chirping songs
As if intrigued by the new rhythm of the machines
That smooth and tame our carpets of grass.
Holding my morning cup of coffee, I step outside
To enjoy my lovely view – woods, plants, flowers.

One worker quickens his pace to catch up with the others,
And he looks up, wiping drops of sweat that roll down
His forehead as he leans on his machine. I take a breath,
And wave tentatively, and in my "pigeon" Spanish I say:
"Muchas gracias. Es muy bonita aqui". And he, puzzled at first,
Smiles and waves back, still riding his machine.

The World According To Marion

There can be flowers that sway in the breeze,
Aware of their beauty they are eager to please,
There can be music to gladden my heart
And I'll listen to Springsteen as well as Mozart.

There can be theatre to broaden my mind
And open my eyes to all of mankind.
There needs to be books about people and places
With unusual customs and quite different faces

There should be children whether quiet or wild,
What a genius whoever invented a child
And there should be blue skies but sometimes some rain,
And I will be grateful and never complain.

I'll allow it to snow for one day at best
But I'll order warm seasons for all of the rest
All of these gifts help my dream world come true,
But, most of all, there has to be you

How I Learned To Swim

My grandchild asks, "Nona, how did you learn to swim?"

I can recall every detail of it – salty taste of ocean, grittiness of sand.
I smile and tell her "I'll show you a photo of the day I learned to swim". Looking at it, taken so long ago, I wonder how I can remember this childhood afternoon and the aunt who died too young, who taught me to swim.

It's summer at Rockaway Beach and I am almost four. I splash in the surf, but only up to my knees, my Mother watching near. And then, suddenly, a rip pulls me off my feet and I'm sucked under, white swirls of foam rushing over me. My mother, afraid of deep water, never a swimmer, somehow grabs me but her panic is contagious and I wail, "Take me out, I don't like the ocean, take me out"!

Back at the blanket I whimper for sympathy until Aunt Becky says,
"Lilly, put her down. You're spoiling her. She needs to learn to swim!" My grandchild nods and smiles.
"Come, she says, the strict aunt who holds out her hand impatiently. I take it, still sputtering but not daring to disobey as she strolls to the ocean. I shuffle my feet through the hot sand, then back in the waves, no rips in sight. Still sniffling I follow her orders.
"I'll twirl you around and you'll see that it's fun, but you can only hold my pinky finger, that's the rule, and you must paddle. Use your other arm and, of course, don't forget to kick your feet."

Slowly Aunt Becky twirls me. I try to grab more fingers but it's no use.
"Remember," She says, "One finger." I paddle more and start to feel the rhythm of it.
I circle round and round, grasping only her pinky, calling "This is fun! It's easy!"
But suddenly Aunt Becky steps back, sliding her finger, my lifeline, away.
I can still feel the shock of this betrayal as I try not to sink, paddling like crazy!
(My grandchild's mouth opens, her eyes widen, she moves closer)

Quickly Aunt Becky calls to me, "Keep paddling, keep kicking, you're fine!"
She smiles, and there I go! I'm in too deep to give up now…I'M SWIMMING!

My grandchild smiles and says "Can you teach me like Aunt Becky?"
I think about how this Aunt, had she lived, might have showed me all the ways to swim through life's dangerous currents or even float and ride the riptides out.
"Yes", I say. "I'll try to teach you everything ".

How To Write! (As Explained By The NY Times!)

I recently read, in the book section of The New York Times, two articles that are "tongue in cheek" but also intriguing as a guide to following your own rules of writing. One of them that immediately caught my eye was, 'Don't go searching for a subject; rather, let the subject find you.' Hm.m.m.m! I sat at the computer wishing that some magical gift from the heavens will immediately inspire me and I will turn out a 'bestseller' within a few minutes.

The well-known advice to 'write what you know' may be a wonderful or a terrible idea. The author suggests that if your heart seems to assure you that what you know is really, really true, and then go with it!

Next we need to consider the vexing and torturous condition of the dreaded "writer's block! If necessary you can fake some terrible event like 'the dog ate my soon-to-be Nobel Prize winning novel!' you might even get away with this (for a short time).

The usual advice given to would-be writers is 'revise!' according to the experts, that's no good; it's simply doing what you should do before you 'revised'! But if you love hundreds of drafts, ok, go for it! Last, there are really no rules - only what you invent for yourself. And you know what? There are many of you with wonderful writing talent.

Anise Singer

For my husband, Howard,
of blessed memory,
whose love and untimely passing,
led me to the 'Magic Room.'
He is, and will always be,
my continued source of creativity
and inspiration.
I pray that the earth rest easy on him.

Birch

You bear the weight of winter,
Nature's enigma

Burdened with iced beauty,
Unwillingly yielding

As Winter presses his weight
Onto each branch,
Your tears shimmer in icy pain

Enduring.

The ground touches your tallest leaf.

You lie there, bent in frozen whiteness
Next to your partner in grief
Under winter's whim
Silent and still
Until life giving Spring
Unfolds relief

Shredding

I sit here
Shredding the history
Of your illness.
Each page takes me back…
Revisiting each appointment
New medications
Tests and scans.
In heart wrenching rhythms
Another piece of paper
Morphs into strips
Shattering the dreams
Of forever together.
I am not halfway done
The notebook, once meticulously
Annotated, memorializing,
The pages of our journey
Is now like leaves in the wind.
Every appointment
Cyber search
More questions than answers.
Day by day
As your life force depleted
I was your cheerleader, chronicler

Despondency carefully
Disguised in between
The pages of our lives,
Twenty two long, but grateful
Months
Now part of a rended history.

Pathways

It was the end of December
When we finally moved in
The year that ended
with Begin.

So reluctant, I balked with a sigh,
This is the place where elephants die.
A decade we had of newfound bliss
No stairs to climb,
No lawns to mow, this is where
The elephants go.

But elephants, you know
Have close family ties,
They remember without judgment where
Their family abides.

Bonding with families and strangers too,
They are passive, and aggressive, protective
Teach relationships,
Protect their young,
Mourn for their losses,
When day is done.

They are very much like us,
As I have come to know.
So I will continue to live where the elephants go.

"Elephants are well-known for their intelligence, close family ties and social complexity, and they remember for years other individuals and places. They live in a fluid fission-fusion society with relationships radiating out from the mother-offspring bond through families, bond groups, clans, independent males and beyond to strangers."

The Poet

More than her poetry
Way beyond my new age understanding
I admire her accomplishments
At only forty one.
Her vitae
Harvard, Stanford, Princeton
Charm, beauty, Caramel skin,
Smiling, reading.
She holds me captive
Does my own poetry get lost in hers?

With grace and dignity
She passes her fingers over her
Dripping nose
Apologizing for her allergies

Her words ebb and flow
With the rhythm of her voice
A joy to watch and hear,
Except for the sniffles and the wipes
Being videotaped for posterity.
Someone hands her a tissue
My mind begins to wander
How will she view herself
In the virtual world
When these visions are recorded?
I find myself cringing
With the thought of purchasing
A book
Signed with the hands that wiped her nose
Berating myself for being so critical
Of one so beautiful and accomplished.

Driving With My Daughter

My achy breaky body woke me at first light
A *zip line* trip to Boston and back
Two days I held on tight
Challenging my muscles and my brain
Daughter's driving nearly drove me insane.
Four wheels a turning, little did I see
As I stared at white knuckles glaring at me!
Five and one half hours each, up and back

My skeleton rebelling
Please cut me some slack!
Back on the highway, the tires just flew
With tension abounding, I was caught in a stew
Of simmering fear and clenching of teeth
'Till we arrived at her house
Such a relief!

My body eased into the driver's seat
Sat back and breathed, such a relief!
Took the scenic shore route, a peaceful ramble,
The motor was purring as we did amble
Through little shore towns, basketed with
Flowers anew, the scent of the sea, the sky so blue.
Pulled into my driveway
Up went the door
Thankful to be back home once more

January 22, 2012

You lie there
Or is it lay?
in inanimate stillness
Death has come and taken you away
Yet, still, you are here
Waiting.

Soon, they will come to prepare you
For your journey.
Our daughter and I
Bend to embrace you one more time.
You leave our room
Warm, in a blanket
It is a visual for us
For you are already in another world.
Stillness, Sadness, Silence
Waft through this air heavy with grief,
Once filled with your voice and laughter.

They are taking you to a holy place
Where prayers and watchful eyes
Make sure that you are not alone.

You requested a simple traditional pine box
I complied.
Our son gifts, his beautiful tallit as your burial shroud
A yarmulke, crocheted by our second daughter
Crowns your proud head with
"Zaide Howie"
Embroidering the memories of when our beloved grandchildren
Became a part of you, your jewels in a crown.

Your memorial service held in the sanctuary of our shul,
In awesome reverence, as nearly 400 people
Came to celebrate your life, and pay tribute
With their own memories.
We laughed because you were a funny guy
We cried because that voice is silenced
We were comforted to see so much love.
We placed you in hallowed ground,
With blessings, tears, and love.

Palm Desert Memoir

The Desert –

Mountainous summits impale blue skies.
Desert palms sway in sunlit air
What is there that can compare?
Eighty degrees melt February's glossy coat.
Where iceberg remnants take my breath away,
I delight in every day.
Houses dot the cliffs close by
Near caves where ancient memories lie.
Oh, blessed friends, whose generosity
Transported me with loving care,
How grateful I am that they brought me here
To where loneliness recedes.

The Shift –

Clouds darken over snowcapped mountainous peaks,
Windmill farms, where mechanical daisies propel
A synchronous dance of wind driven synergy
Planted among the desert rocks, peacefully strewn in earth colors.
Suddenly, blatant commercialism invades this peaceful plane,

Obstructing our vision.
The calm I photographed by my mind's eye
Dissipates, contaminating the vista,
Intrusive, beckoning, seductive.
Life, for the moment is reduced to a bargain,
Recalling emotions of this past year, when I tried to bargain with G-d.
Suddenly, the skies open, and the unexpected rains came.

The Cactus –

Loneliness invades.
Handholding couples sit around the breakfast table,
A Noah's ark.
Oblivious to the spoke that doesn't fit
like a like a cactus spine it pierces my heart,
I reflect on his words to me:
"It's not fair."
To miss someone so badly is beyond hurt,
To remember the words you wanted to say, but were

Never said. The more hugs you wanted to give and couldn't
The "I love you's" were abundant.
One more week, and I leave the warm skies of Palm Desert
To the cold warmth of home.
I behold the sun streaked sky this morning,
Dressed in purple hues.

Again, a stem of a cactus needle pierces my heart,
And made it bleed tears.
It was she, the intruder.
A thunderous mountain of flesh,
Self-absorbed, narcissistic, perhaps self-loathing woman, from Las Vegas,
Who spewed the glory of her show business past
She drank coffee with her pinkie curled in the air.
She was the suffocating oil to my water
They were friends of their friends. I held my breath until I was
Unable to breathe, and exited the breakfast to the solitude
Of my own space, where my tears flowed down like rain,
Releasing me from pent up grief.
They finally left, and I walked back out into the sunbaked desert,
Feeling, once again, blessed to be embraced
by a world of beauty and friendship.

The Art of War

The sun is shining.
Morning eyes drift across the pages of
Blurred gray
Arts and Leisure
Senses suddenly jarred
By the vicissitudes of war.
Art that captures the horrors of
Human spoils in torment
A visual telling by artists whose penciled lines trace
The long path of rehabilitation for
Wounded Warriors
An innocuous state at first glance suddenly turns
Into an indictment.
Here the sketches graphically illustrate
Loss of limbs
Tattoos and Tubes
Stretched on a canvas of pain.
Here are the 'Portraits of War.'
Morning suddenly shifts to mourning.
The pencil moves our eyes erratically
Following each movement,
Dramatically capturing the pain and reality of every stroke--
Pencils seemingly pierce a soldier's half closed eyes
Inward reflecting the paths of memory
No need to read the text,
Verbs and adjectives do not command the viewer's eyes.
The artist is the purveyor of truth,
Legislating the legitimacy of War.

The Clock

It is steaming today.
Ninety-four degrees and rising
Relieved, I pull into the shelter
Of the garage, and the
quiet of home.
The leather sofa provides
A cool respite as
My body sinks
Into its welcoming softness.
My head limps back
Cradled by the cushion.
Breathing deeply, I close my eyes
To the absolute silence surrounding me
  Like amniotic fluid.
I hear it…
  TICK TOCK, TICK TOCK
My eyes open,
  TICK TOCK,
To focus on the golden
Beauty of the Tiffany clock
Our children presented to us
On the occasion of our
Thirtieth wedding anniversary.
  TICK TOCK
I lift it
From its home on the shelf where it has stood
For the past twenty years.
Turning it,
  TICK TOCK
To read the inscription:
  Happy 30th anniversary
  Mom and dad
  With love and respect
  Esta, Brad and Estera
" i am through you so i "

The line leads to the little knob that opens the door
To the inner workings of our lives.
  TICK TOCK, TICK TOCK…
Fifty years of seconds slowly ticked and tucked

Into the words of the poet
Of how we lived our lives…
Now signaling the seconds, minutes, days, and years
That I must spend without you…
Still
      TICK TOCK

 i am through you so I
* e. e. cummings   "i am so glad and very…"

My Grandparent's Apartment

The dining room table was enormous, but then everything loomed large above the eyes of a four-year old. Its length stretched expansively across the living room of the tiny apartment. It was embraced by high backed upholstered Jacobean style chairs, much too large for the small family from Odessa that graced the dinners that filled the apartment with aromas from another place and time.

The table's legs, much bigger than my small frame, carved from substantial mahogany, created a cavernous world where I could escape from the grown-up gatherings and still be privy to the dialogue above me. Then, one day it was gone. Too big for the tiny space-- a dinette table with fours chairs stood in its stead. A light colored oak now placed against the fire place window where grandpa could sit and wait for us to come from faraway New Jersey. Our car, whose putt, putt sound was challenged by the roar of the Pelham Parkway El, seemed to struggle up the hill to meet my grandfather's face framed in that very window.

From the old dining room set, two giant arm chairs remained, pressed against the wall; arms incapable of wrapping my tiny frame. I played on the floral linoleum amid the company of feet, and the cacophony of the language I did not know. I was relieved to see that the china closet still dominated the far wall, for behind its keyed door, among the crystal decanters of my grandfather's own fermenting schnapps, was the Nescafe jar filled with Roosevelt dimes that grandma filled from one visit to the next. It became a ritual each time as I, and eventually my brother, stood silently and waited patiently as the tiny coins were divided between us.

The radio remained in the corner and on rare visits, over the years, Grandma and I shared the adventures of Stella Dallas, and Helen Trent, as she ironed and I played. The sofa had changed, as in its place stood one of the first Castros'. I couldn't open it myself, but when I was left to stay and play, I became a "princess" to the parents of my father. At times I would bounce and turn and whirl until I felt I would "turn into butter" like the tiger in story now out of print.

At the break of dawn, my grandmother would wake me, and we would walk to the street where the aromas of fresh ethnic foods invited us into those wonderful shops that have now been replaced by enormous supermarkets containing foods in Styrofoam trays and plastic casings. My grandmother would carefully shop for the fresh bread, chickens, and vegetables ---she was a woman who would not take less than the best.

The kitchen was a hidden space. High doors concealed the tiny Frigidaire, and the sink with its blue and white kosher soap, the stove and the magic table that grew out of the opened door. It balanced on one unfolded leg, revealing the secrets to the preparation of that wonderful food. I think now that the table was probably an outgrowth of the Murphy bed concept, and the precursor to the modular units of today's eclectic world. On this table was placed a large wooden bowl, a hand chopper, and a meat grinder that commanded my eyes to be glued to the bloody red spaghetti-like substance that squeezed through its tiny portals, producing the meat that would become the world's juiciest hamburgers.

The foyer was the most seductive place of all. Huge photographs of ancient faces hung in carved frames that a junk dealer would eventually claim for a fee. The trunk held the stories of generations from the treacherous trip across the ocean from Odessa to Ellis Island. The curve of its lid provided a slide for my young bottom, providing that one could scale its side to the crest. Next was the credenza, the very last remnant of the dining room set. It sat against the wall. Its massive legs held drawers of fabric which my grandmother collected, material which would magically evolve into the latest fashions. From her nimble fingers also came hundreds of aprons which she would sell to raise money for the construction of the Workmen's Circle Home.

I could sit for hours and watch her feet working the wrought iron pedal, as her fingers pushed the fabric into the moving needle. I delighted in the bobbin process -- the large spool on top giving birth to the thread in the shiny metal disc that was hidden in the secret little compartment that magically seamed the work of my grandmother's hands. I never learned to sew.

The bedroom is as clear in my mind as a picture on my wall today. Dark, delicious wood, polished and bright as the mirror above the dresser that reflected the lives of the couple that stand in the history of my childhood. My grandfather's armoire, housing his too few suits, fascinated me. Its little door opened to reveal a tiny cave, big enough for a four year old to cause a grandparent some anxious moments. I could not see the photographs perched atop, but I knew they were there. The bed presented the biggest challenge--the climb to the snowy sheets and the billowy pillows that cradled my dreams, under an embankment of feathers. I remember the comfort of sleeping in my grandparent's bed and listening to the rattle of the steam escaping from the radiator., giving the heat that would warm the rooms and dry the hand laundry. The vanity evoked my little girl curiosity, as I moved its two hinged mirrors back and forth to see myself cloned, ad infinitum. These were the days of remembrance and fantasy, of playing grown-up and exploring my grandparent's treasures.

I would be remiss if I didn't tell about the bathroom. Ipana and Cue side by side, and a container that held a set of teeth. My favorite fixture was the four-legged bathtub, where I played forever until my grandmother's hands squeezed the warm water over my body and wrapped me in the world's largest towel. Then, she would bring in his wonderful bottle of oil -- a fragrance I have never forgotten, which even today evokes a nostalgic smile. Olive oil. She proceeded to rub it into my skin until I glowed warm.

Many years later, as a young bride searching for a new recipe, I came across the two familiar words, which in this context did not make sense....cooking with bath oil? I was long to use it, but eventually did and smiled one summer when a trip to Italy challenged my memory once again.

The apartment is still there in the Bronx. Who lives there? I don't know. The furniture was extracted by a junk dealer whom my father paid to haul its mahogany bulk down to the streets below. I have seen that furniture time and time again in the yesterday stores. The photographs of my great grandparents are gone, along with the carved frames that embraced their ancient faces. They probably grace the walls in somebody's mansion. Gone are the crystal decanters that held my grandfather's schnapps, and the Nescafe jars with the Roosevelt dimes. I have the sewing machine, converted to electric at some point in time, and a porcelain cereal set from Czechoslovakia, which my aunt remembered that I loved as a child, and saved for me.

I have my memories which sometimes hide too deeply in the recesses of my soul, and sometimes, like now, they surface so that someday my children and grandchildren can live in my grandparent's apartment.

About the Contributing Writers

Rosalie Auerbach – For many years Rosalie taught reading and writing at many grade levels. The last twenty years, she taught high school creative writing, where she once again found the path to writing that she had lost along the way.

Lydia Bargiuk – Ever since Lydia was a young adult, she was a lover of the creative arts. They were a perfect complement to her pursuit of mathematics and physical sciences. Her poems reflect her passion for the visual arts

Phil de Anguera – Phil's lifelong fascination with spiritual philosophy has inspired a variety of short written pictures of his ideals, reflections and conclusions

Marygene Coleman Fagan – Marygene began writing with a love of the English language and by immersing herself with poetry and a mentorship with a published author. Her education and profession as an English teacher in the United States, Europe and Asia allowed her to expand her writing to fiction and non-fiction and she was acknowledged for her work in developing writing with young students. Marygene's extensive travel, meeting with citizens of numerous countries and her love of Africa and its animals allow her love of writing to remain vibrant, unique, and passionate.

John Patrick Gatton – Patrick's first poem titled, "*Imagine*," was written to create lovely images of the arrival of his daughter Cynthia Jean in Heaven after a fatal auto accident. The joyful subject of the poem confirmed that life is eternal and beautiful. For thirty years it has stimulated his continued writing of more than eight hundred poems.

Elaine Grassi – Sadly, Elaine passed before this book could be published. Her daughter, Christina Grassi Pierson, writes about her mother - 'I cannot remember a time in my life when I didn't think of my mother as a poet and someone with a gift for words. She started writing poetry in her youth, during her teenage years, and has used it throughout her life for many purposes. But I think her final decade was the most prolific and meaningful. Primarily her work has to do with reflection: reflection on the world, or religion, but primarily her poetry is a reflection on her life. She truly had a gift that she honed into an art. Her quote, "The task of the poet is to arrange skillfully the words that life has spoken to her" are her words and demonstrates her perspective about writing. She felt she had to be inspired and luckily for us, many things inspired her.'

Fran Karnish – Fran is the original mentor and advisor to the writers herein. She also taught first and second grades, was a ghost writer and also wrote speeches for a senator. She started a ministry with her husband when in her 30's and established a home for seniors. Her faith is extraordinary and her lifelong care for others is reflected in her writing.

Barbara Pastorello – Barbara graduated with commercial honors and academic diplomas in 1957. Was accepted to NYU and worked at the Graduate School as faculty secretary and for the Chairman of the Economics Dept. She started writing in grammar school and never stopped. Writing soothes her, inspired her and gives her peace of mind.

Joan Saunders (Editor) – Joan's love of poetry began at a very early age, when she carried around Robert Lewis Stephenson's, *A Childs Garden of Verses* and stood on the kitchen table, reciting the poems from memory, for anyone who would listen. She began writing poetry herself 15 years ago, and since then, it has become a constant passion. In her writing, she draws on her diverse life experiences – born and raised in England and now residing in America. She has studied poetry writing for many years with well-known poets – Marge Piercy, Billy Collins and a host of others and she also provides poetry workshops in her own home, to encourage poetry writing in others. Joan is also the editor of this collection of poetry and prose.

Marion Stavitsky – When Marion was a child, her parents loved to teach her the old Russian poems from their own childhood in Minsk and Borisov. This developed in her a strong appreciation for poetry of all kinds. As a high school English teacher, she would read poetry to her students and encourage them to write their own. She believes that reading and writing poetry can be a catharsis for anyone.

Anise Winokur Singer – Anise feels that she has been writing forever. Certainly, from her teenage years. Often, underneath the sheets with her diary and a flashlight, words flowed from pen to paper. She sometimes wrote in the darkness of night, standing at her window, using the moonlight. During a time of great personal sadness, she became a part of the writers group. Or, as she says, healer's group! The writers in this anthology formed, not just a group, but a bond, where we share our thoughts in poetry and prose, and roundtable critiques. It has been a blessing to Anise.

Made in the USA
Charleston, SC
20 October 2015